GERMAN-ENGLISH FALSE FRIENDS
Reference and Practice

Book 3

GEOFF PARKES and ALAN CORNELL

illustrated by ULI STURM

SOUTHAMPTON

ENGLANG BOOKS,
P.O.Box 240,
Southampton SO9 7RJ,
England.

© Englang Books 1993

First published 1993

ISBN 1 871819 25 3   German-English False Friends (Book 3)

Also available in this series:

ISBN 1 871819 20 2   German-English False Friends (Book 1) 2nd edition
ISBN 1 871819 15 6   German-English False Friends (Book 2)
ISBN 1 871819 10 5   101 Myths About The English Language

In Preparation:

How To Pronounce It: A Guide to Words With Disputed Pronunciations
Prepositions

All rights reserved. No part of this publication may be reproduced, stored in a retrieval system, or transmitted, in any form or by any means, electronic, magnetic tape, electrostatic, photocopying, recording, mechanical, or otherwise, without the prior permission of Englang Books in writing.

British Library Cataloguing in Publication Data

Parkes, Geoff
    German-English False Friends. - Book 3:
    Reference and Practice
    I. Title II. Cornell, Alan
    430.1

ISBN 1-871819-25-3

Typeset by Englang Books
Printed and bound in Great Britain by Hobbs The Printers, Southampton

CONTENTS

Acknowledgments		4
List of Abbreviations		5
Introduction		6
Section A	absolvieren - blank	10
Section A	Exercises	21
Section B	Blende - Ebbe	23
Section B	Exercises	36
Section C	enorm - Frontal-	38
Section C	Exercises	49
Section D	Golf - Jubiläum	51
Section D	Exercises	62
Section E	Justiz - Konzert	64
Section E	Exercises	74
Section F	Korn - Moment	76
Section F	Exercises	86
Section G	Montage - Pflaster	88
Section G	Exercises	98
Section H	Pickel - raffiniert	100
Section H	Exercises	111
Section I	Rakete - schwimmen	113
Section I	Exercises	126
Section J	schwindeln - Testament	128
Section J	Exercises	141
Section K	Tick - zivil / Zivil	143
Section K	Exercises	152
Section L	Short Entries: Achsel - Zylinder	154
Section L	Test	174
Section M	Pseudo-Anglicisms: Aircondition - Whirlpool	177
Final Test	Final Test	185
Key to Exercises and Tests		192
Index to Books 1, 2 and 3		202

ACKNOWLEDGMENTS

Sincere thanks are due to the following, who read and discussed various drafts of the book and who made numerous suggestions for improvements: Susanne Austmann, Beatrix Beyerle, Therese Biedl, Frank Chen, Bernhard Eidel, Beate Elsen, Rudolf Erndl, Katharina Faber, Maren Freitag, Anetta Gänsler-Parkes, Christoph Gross, Ralf Gross, Regine Gläser, Vera Görgen, Georg Gottschalk, Martin Gussmann, Jörg Hülsken, Romana Jansen, Silke Kammer, Anke van Kempen, Susanne Krauthäuser, Daniela Lange, Karen Levecke, Manuela von Papen, Marcus Pleyer, Arno Rauschenbeutel, Bernhard Rauscher, Tom Reinhold, Petra Specht, Bettina Stangl, Matthias Strauch, Gabriele Strzybny, Frithjof Weber, Frank Wienand, Sylvia Wille, Ursula Zinschitz. Thanks are also due to Chris Perkins for substantial help during the early stages of the project.

For help with Swiss usage, we are particularly indebted to Franz Fries, Marianne Süsli and Dr. Adolf Meister and family.

As usual, our richest source of inspiration has been the fund of false friends problems provided by, and discussed with, our students. They are drawn from the whole of the German-speaking world, but we especially have to thank those attending the following institutions: Southampton English Language Centre; the Universities of Erlangen, Bonn, Zürich, Vienna, Göttingen, Regensburg, Würzburg, Stuttgart, Heidelberg, Duisburg, Braunschweig, Düsseldorf and Bremen; the Pädagogische Hochschulen of Weingarten and Freiburg.

LIST OF ABBREVIATIONS

abbreviation	German	English
adj.	Adjektiv	adjective
allg.	allgemein	general
AmE	amerikanisches Englisch	American English
ärztl., med.	ärztlich, medizinisch	medical
bes.	besonders	especially
biol.	biologisch	biological
Bot.	Botanik	Botany
BrE	britisches Englisch	British English
cf., vgl.	vergleiche	compare
chem.	chemisch	chemical
coll., ugs.	umgangssprachlich	colloquial
comm., econ.	wirtschaftlich	commercial, economic
cul.	kulinarisch	culinary
d.h.	das heißt	that is
dt., G	deutsch	German
E, engl.	englisch	English
etc., usw.	und so weiter	etcetera
fin.	finanziell	financial
form.	formell	formal
Foto.	Fotographie	photography
geog.	geographisch	geographical
geol.	geologisch	geological
geom.	geometrisch	geometrical
gramm.	grammatikalisch	grammatical
hist.	historisch	historical
intrans.	intransitiv	intransitive
jmd., jmdn., jmdm.	jemand, jemanden, jemandem	someone
jur.	juristisch	legal
lit.	literarisch	literary
math.	mathematisch	mathematical
mil.	militärisch	military
mus.	musikalisch	musical
Myth.	Mythologie	mythology
n.	Substantiv	noun
N.B.	nota bene	nota bene (note well)
Opt.	Optik	Optics
orn.	ornithologisch	ornithological
o.s.	sich	oneself
Pl.	Plural	plural
pol.	politisch	political
relig.	religiös	religious
sex.	sexuell	sexual
s.o.	jemand	someone
s.th.	etwas	something
Sw.	schweizerisch	Swiss usage
tech.	technisch	technical
theat.	Theater	theatrical
trans.	transitiv	transitive
u.ä.	und ähnliche(s)	and similar
übertr.	übertragen	figurative, metaphorical
u.U.	unter Umständen	possibly
v.	Verb	verb
Zool.	Zoologie	Zoology

INTRODUCTION

Since you are reading this, the introduction to the third and highest-level volume in a series of three books, you are probably very competent at English, have waded through one or both of the preceding volumes, and are well aware of the meaning of *false friends*. However, for those who have jumped straight in at Book 3, allow us to recapitulate: false friends are pairs of words in two (or more) languages which look similar but which have different meanings either all of the time (total false friends) or part of the time (partial false friends). The vast majority are partial false friends. Examples of total false friends in this volume are *Akkord / accord, Branche / branch, Crux / crux, personell / personal*, and *skurril / scurrilous*. Examples of partial false friends are: *Drachen / dragon, Fieber / fever, schizophren / schizophrenic , solide / solid*, and *human / humane*.

The agonies of selection

Book 1 (second edition) contains 116 false friends pairs essential for any German speaker learning English. Book 2 follows on with a further 112 pairs - still indispensable for anyone dealing with English in depth. Relatively speaking, the selection of these 228 was not difficult: we had been bombarded with them in classrooms for years and the items shouted to be included.

Book 3 was a different kettle of fish. Not counting the 228 already covered, we still had nearly 2000 pairs to choose from for this volume! Since we assumed that readers would not want to struggle through 800 pages, our selection problem assumed a magnitude we had not previously encountered. One result is that we are painfully aware of the hundreds of pairs we have had to leave out. At the same time, we have gone to great lengths to ensure that our readers are not burdened with items so rare or so esoteric that they would be of hardly any use. Throughout this series, our guiding light has been *usefulness*.

The main body of this book follows the tried-and-tested pattern of the first two volumes. The fact that the last sections are different in style is a result of the rigorous selection procedure mentioned above. After the main text, containing 224 pairs, we include a 'Short Items' Section, with a further 135 pairs. These 135 items are no less important than the preceding 224, but they are more straightforward, and less in need of lengthy explanations. In many cases they are simple nouns with easily understandable, direct equivalents, e.g. *der Schellfisch* = haddock; *shellfish* = Schaltier; Meeresfrüchte. This section therefore contains no example sentences, but we do include useful associated phrases and idioms.

Following the 'Short Items', we include a Section with 93 'Pseudo-anglicisms' - a group which has not figured in previous volumes. These are English, partly English, or English-looking expressions which have been incorporated into the German language but which cannot be used in the same way in English. Some of them function just like the false friends in the main body of the book, in which case we have given them similar - if somewhat shorter - treatment. But many of them do not exist at all in English, and here we have tried to pinpoint the nearest English equivalents.

The changing status of false friends

Language is about as static as a quicksand. Words come and go, become more or less fashionable, or sometimes change their meanings. False friends are as susceptible to changes in meaning as any other vocabulary items - perhaps more so. Let's look at three examples of pairs which are false friends now, but may not be for very much longer.

The first obvious example is **sympathisch / sympathetic** (Book 1). We know that the normal translation of *sympathisch* is *nice, pleasant*, or *likeable*, and that the normal translation of *sympathetic* is *mitfühlend*. Yet one now regularly hears native English speakers saying "I really liked that chap Dave - he was really *sympathetic* " - when there isn't a broken leg or a broken marriage in sight. Why? One theory goes like this:

"People travel abroad more these days. They've been doing so ever since package holidays became popular in the 60s. Since most native English speakers aren't brilliant at foreign languages, they tend to conduct conversations with others (often Europeans) in English. Some English vocabulary mistakes are the same in many European countries, so native speakers hear them hundreds of times. They pick them up, import them into Britain, America, etc., and start using them at home in the foreign sense. And there we have it."

For *sympathisch / sympathetic*, the logic of this argument is difficult to refute. Look at the word in four major European languages:

German	*sympathisch*	French	*sympathique*
Spanish	*simpàtico*	Italian	*simpatico*

English is clearly the odd man out. Has this (relatively) new use been imported unwittingly as indicated above? Or is there perhaps in some circles a less subconscious feeling that "if the British don't use the word like this yet, then at least they ought to!"? We shall probably never know, but whatever the answer, the fact remains that this pair stands a good chance of not being false friends at all in 20 or 30 years.

Let's look next at **Objektiv / objective** (Book 3). The standard equivalents are not in dispute: *Objektiv* = lens; *objective* = Ziel. In fact the English word *objective* is already used as a technical expression by opticians and astronomers, who describe the lens nearest the object being observed as *the objective lens* or simply *the objective*. Up to now, the word in this sense has languished in almost total obscurity as far as the general public is concerned. Yet it is now creeping into photographic magazines in the German sense: "This new ultra-wide-angle from Klikon really is a beautiful *objective*." It has a long way to go before it can compete, in usage terms, with *sympathetic*, but photography is one of Britain's favourite hobbies, and photography magazines sell like hot cakes. Could this usage too be the start of a trend?

Finally, consider an example from our **Pseudo-anglicisms** section in this volume: **Slip / slip**. German *Slip* = briefs / (under)pants / knickers (see p.183). A good English-English dictionary will list 15 - 20 meanings for *slip* (most frequent translations would be *Unterrock* and *Flüchtigkeitsfehler*) but *briefs* would not normally be among them. Nevertheless, the word is now sometimes to be found on underwear packaging, especially for men's briefs; it has a good chance of becoming a true friend.

Disguised false friends

A special word of warning is necessary about false friends whose difficulty is not immediately detectable. If you work through this book in the normal way, you will start by looking at the *German* half of a pair and quickly see that it is not translatable by its obvious counterpart: *absolvieren* can't be translated by *absolve*; *Blende* cannot be translated by *blend*; *mondän* cannot be translated by *mundane*, etc. But it doesn't always work like that. G *Argument* = E *argument* ; G *Garage* = E *garage* ; G *realisieren* = E *realise*. So where's the problem?

The problem is that sometimes you discover the false friend only when you start from the *English* . In the above three examples, it is the *English* word which is ambiguous, not the German:

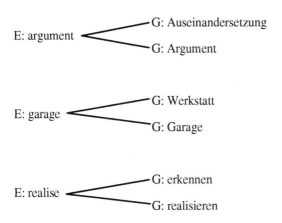

It pays to watch out for this category of false friend, which is often overlooked.

How to use this book

Readers of previous volumes know that we recommend you to work through the book methodically from start to finish, since the exercises are arranged cyclically. However, you may experience more of a desire to chop and change with this volume. If you feel such a desire, yield to it! Also, do give your memories a chance; if you get stuck with an exercise, or in the tests, don't fly to the Key for help without racking your brains thoroughly beforehand. You are more likely to remember a difficult item if you have had to puzzle over it for a while first. The philosophy in the false friends volumes is the same as the philosophy in the gym: no gain without pain!

Explanations

The language of explanations and definitions in this book switches - deliberately - between English and German. In the main body of entries we have stuck to German in an attempt to be user-friendly at difficult times, but you will find English used extensively in other places, notably the Pseudo-anglicisms Section.

And what of the future?

There is unlikely to be a Book 4. "The Return of False Friends" might turn into "Nightmare on Vocabulary Street", and we would feel terribly guilty about causing people loss of sleep. In any case, once you have really mastered the 680 items in these three books, you will probably feel like moving on to something else. That does not mean we have stopped collecting pairs (two more were found skulking in a business magazine this very week!), and it does not mean that we do not want to hear from you any more. Readers' and teachers' comments have proved invaluable over the years, and can continue to do so in influencing future editions of these volumes. Once again, our sincerest thanks go to all those who have written in with comments and suggestions.

Note on pronunciation

We have kept to the transcription system of Gimson's *English Pronouncing Dictionary* - EPD - (14th edition, 1977), with one major exception: the close vowel in the final segment of words such as *city, pretty* is transcribed with /i/, not /ɪ/: /'sɪti/, /'prɪti/. This is now standard practice among phoneticians (see Wells's *Longman Pronunciation Dictionary*, 1990 - LPD - and Roach's *English Phonetics and Phonology*, 1985), and eliminates transcriptions such as /'prɪtɪ/ for *pretty*, where the use of the one symbol /ɪ/ for two different sounds is clearly illogical and misleading.

As far as recommended versions are concerned, ours are almost identical to those in LPD, which nowadays offers a more accurate description of modern standard English (RP) than EPD does. However, in a very small number of cases, our own research* indicates that even the LPD occasionally lists as first versions what are in fact almost certainly minority versions, and here our listings differ in minor respects from theirs. These small differences are almost exclusively confined to vowel quality in unstressed syllables.

Finally, we have tried not to burden the reader with too many unnecessary alternative listings. Thus, for example, an optional svar /ə/ is often omitted from our transcriptions altogether in words where it is very unlikely to be pronounced.

Southampton, May 1993

---

*detailed recordings, carried out at the BBC, other studios, and various other locations in southern England for *How To Pronounce It* (Englang Books)

SECTION A

ABSOLVIEREN / ABSOLVE

G *absolvieren:* (ableisten, erledigen, verrichten: Lehrgang, Übungen usw.) to complete, take, do, work

Jedes Jahr **absolviere** ich einen Fortbildungskurs.	*Every year I **take** an in-service training course.*
Von den 200 Studierenden, die diesen Studiengang aufnahmen, **absolvierten** ihn nur 40.	*Of the 200 students who began this course, only 40 **completed** it.*
Wir mußten alle zehn Runden **absolvieren**.	*We all had to **do/complete** ten laps.*
In der Fabrik mußte er einen Zehnstundentag **absolvieren**.	*He had to **do/work** a ten-hour day at the factory.*

E *absolve* /əb'zɒlv/: (von Schuld, Sünden, Verpflichtung, usw.) freisprechen, lossprechen

The priest **absolved** him from his sins.	*Der Priester **sprach** ihn von seinen Sünden **frei/los**.*

AGGREGAT / AGGREGATE

G *Aggregat:*   1. (tech.) unit; (für elektrischen Strom) generator
                2. (geol.) aggregate

1. | | |
   |---|---|
   | Das **Kühlaggregat** muß regelmäßig gewartet werden. | *The refrigeration **unit** must be serviced regularly.* |
   | Das ganze **Bremsaggregat** war defekt. | *The whole brake-**unit** was faulty.* |
   | In unserer Hütte waren wir letztes Wochenende auf Kerzen angewiesen, da unser **Aggregat** ausgefallen war. | *In our hut last weekend we had to rely on candles, as our **generator** wasn't working.* |

E *aggregate* /'ægrɪgət/: 1. Summe, Gesamtmenge; Gesamt-
                              2. (Bestandteil von Beton) Zuschlagstoffe

1. | | |
   |---|---|
   | The **aggregate** for this year's maintenance costs is far higher than we thought. | *Die diesjährigen **Gesamtkosten** für Instandhaltung sind viel höher, als wir uns gedacht hatten.* |

Leeds lost 2-0* to Bremen in Germany, but since they beat Bremen 3-0 at home, they win 3-2 **on aggregate**.

*In Deutschland verlor Leeds mit 0:2 gegen Bremen, da sie aber im Heimspiel Bremen 3:0 schlugen, gewinnen sie mit **insgesamt** 3:2.*

* *pronounced "two-nil" - and written 2-0 (**not** 0-2) in English.*

AKADEMIKER(IN) / ACADEMIC

G *Akademiker(in):* (Person mit abgeschlossener Hochschulbildung) (university etc.) graduate

Akademiker verdienen im Durchschnitt viel mehr.

(*University*) *graduates* earn much more on average.

E *academic:* Dozent(in), Hochschullehrer(in) (bes. im Plural; manchmal mit der leicht negativen Bedeutung des Weltfremden)

What do **academics** like you know about the problems of an entrepreneur?

*Was wissen denn **Hochschullehrer** wie Sie über die Probleme eines Unternehmers?*

AKKORD / ACCORD

G *Akkord:* 1. (Bezahlungsmodalität) piecework; (Satz) piece(work) rate
2. (mus.) chord

1. Alle diese Frauen arbeiten im **Akkord**.

   *All these women do **piecework** / are on **piecework**.*

   Die können nicht einfach mir nichts, dir nichts den **Akkord** herabsetzen.

   *They can't just put down the **piece rate** without so much as a by-your-leave.*

2. Dieser **Akkord** signalisiert den Übergang zur Moll-Tonart.

   *This **chord** marks the shift to the minor key.*

E *accord* /ə'kɔːd/: 1. (form.) Einigung, Übereinstimmumg
2. of one's own accord: aus freien Stücken

1. The two countries were unable to reach an **accord**.

   *Die beiden Länder konnten keine **Einigung** erzielen.*

2. She gave the money to charity **of her own accord**.   *Sie gab das Geld einer karitativen Einrichtung **aus freien Stücken**.*

AKKURAT / ACCURATE

G *akkurat:*   1. (ordentlich) neat, tidy; (äußerst sorgfältig) meticulous
                   2. (genau) accurate, precise: siehe E *accurate*

1. Ihre Tochter hat eine sehr **akkurate** Handschrift.   *Your daughter has got very **neat** handwriting.*

   Er hält seine Wohnung sehr **akkurat**.   *He keeps his flat very **tidy**.*

   Er ist ein äußerst **akkurater** Mensch.   *He's an extremely **meticulous** person.*

2. Sie hat das Foto sehr **akkurat** auf die Größe des Bilderrahmens zurechtgeschnitten.   *She cut the photo very **precisely** to fit the size of the picture frame.*

E *accurate* /ˈækjərət/:   **genau, präzise**

Such projections are rarely **accurate**.   *Solche Hochrechnungen sind selten **genau**.*

AKTEUR / ACTOR

G *Akteur:*   1. (allgemein: jmd., der in einer bestimmten Situation handelt) participant, person involved, (bes. wichtige Person) protagonist
                 2. (Theater, Film) actor, member of the cast, player
                 3. (Sport) player, member of the team, team member, contestant

1. Die **Akteure** des Geiseldramas wurden über Nacht berühmt.   *Those involved/The participants in this hostage drama became famous overnight.*

E *actor:* **Schauspieler**

ALLÜRE(N) / ALLURE

G *Allüre(n):* (geziertes Verhalten, Starallüren) airs (and graces), affectations

Sie ist eine ganz normale Bürogehilfin und hat doch **(Star)allüren**.
*She's a perfectly ordinary office girl and yet she puts on **airs (and graces)** / **affectations**.*

E *allure* /ə'lʊə/: (form.) Reiz, Attraktion

The **allure** of the scenery lies in its variety.
*Der **Reiz** der Landschaft liegt in ihrer Vielfältigkeit.*

ANIMATEUR(IN) / ANIMATOR

G *Animateur(in):* host(ess), entertainer. Die engl. Äquivalente sind ungenauer als das dt. Wort; bei Pauschalreisen könnte u.u. auch "rep(resentative)" benutzt werden, wenn der/die Betreffende nicht nur die üblichen Reiseleiterfunktionen erfüllt, sondern auch bei stimmungsmachenden Shows u.ä. mitwirkt.

E *animator* /'ænɪmeɪtə/: (Film) Animator(in), Trickzeichner(in)

ANIMIEREN / ANIMATE

G *animieren:* 1. (anregen) to encourage, stimulate, prompt
2. (bei Trickfilmen usw.) to animate

1. Seine Opferbereitschaft hat viele junge Leute dazu **animiert**, für die Wohlfahrt zu arbeiten.
*His willingness to make sacrifices **encouraged** many young people to work for charity.*

E *animate* /'ænɪmeɪt/: 1. beleben
2. vgl. G2.

1. His presence will not exactly **animate** the conversation.
*Seine Anwesenheit wird das Gespräch nicht gerade **beleben**.*

N.B. *To animate* wird als Vollverb relativ selten verwendet; weit häufiger ist das adjektivierte Partizip *animated* = lebhaft, rege - z.B. *an animated discussion* = eine lebhafte Diskussion.

ANTIK / ANTIQUE, ANTIC

G *antik:* 1. (das klassische Altertum betreffend) ancient, classical, in the ancient world
2. (Möbel usw.) antique

1. Über die **antike** Baukunst weiß ich so gut wie nichts.

   I know practically nothing about classical architecture.

   Auch der **antike** Mensch hatte solche Sorgen.

   Ancient man / Man in the ancient world had such troubles, too.

2. **Antike** Möbel sind heute unerschwinglich.

   Antique furniture is prohibitively expensive nowadays.

   Dein Plattenspieler ist wirklich **antik**.

   Your record-player is really antique.

E *antique* /æn'tiːk/: 1. (adj.) siehe G2.
2. (noun) Antiquität - siehe unten

E *antic(s)* / 'æntɪks/ *(noun):* Mätzchen

Stop your childish **antics** and come and help me with the washing-up.

Hör doch auf mit deinen Mätzchen und hilf mir beim Abwaschen.

ANTIQUITÄT / ANTIQUITY

G *Antiquität:* antique / æn'tiːk/

Wer kann sich es heute noch leisten, **Antiquitäten** zu sammeln?

Who can afford to collect antiques nowadays?

E *antiquity* /æn'tɪkwəti/: 1. das Altertum, (griechisch-römisch) die Antike
2. (im Pl.) Altertümer (d.h. Bauwerke aus dem Altertum)
3. großes Alter, Umschreibung mit *sehr alt*, *uralt*.

1. This discovery was already known in **antiquity**.

   Diese Erfindung war schon im Altertum / in der Antike bekannt.

2. The museum is showing a lot of Egyptian **antiquities**.

   Das Museum zeigt viele ägyptische Altertümer.

3. This is a vase of great **antiquity**.   *Es handelt sich hier um eine **sehr alte
                                              Vase**.*

ARREST / ARREST

G *Arrest:* 1. (von Eltern auferlegt) Umschreibung mit *keep in, stay in,
              not allow out, (AmE) 'you're grounded'*.
           2. (mil.) detention; Umschreibung mit *military prison* usw.
           3. (Verhaftung, Festnahme) arrest: siehe E *arrest*

1. "Ich sperre dir das Taschengeld. Außerdem   *"I'm stopping your pocket money. In
   kriegst du zwei Wochen (Haus)**arrest**."   addition **you're going to have to
                                                stay in / you're not going to be
                                                allowed out** for two weeks."*

2. Der Soldat bekam drei Tage **Arrest**.   *The soldier was sentenced to three days
                                             in the **military prison** / the **guard
                                             house**.*

E *arrest* /əˈrest/: Festnahme, Verhaftung, Arrest

You're under **arrest**.   *Sie sind **verhaftet/festgenommen/
                            unter Arrest**.*

The police will soon be making an **arrest**.   *Die Polizei wird bald eine **Verhaftung**
                                                 vornehmen / zu einer **Festnahme**
                                                 schreiten.*

Note: E *house arrest* is used only in the context of political prisoners.

ATTEST, ATTESTIEREN / ATTEST(ATION)

G *Attest:* (ärztl.) medical certificate, doctor's certificate, sick-note

Von Doktor Sommer bekommt man immer   *You can always get a **sick-note** from
ein **Attest**.   Dr. Sommer.*

G *attestieren:* to certify

Verschiedene Ärzte haben ihm seine   *Various doctors have **certified** his
Erwerbsunfähigkeit **attestiert**.   inability to work.*

E *attest* /ə'test/: (Verb, meist mit *to*) bezeugen, bescheinigen, bestätigen

These documents **attested to** the fact that the man was dead.

Diese Unterlagen bezeugten den Tod des Mannes.

E *attestation* /ˌæte'steɪʃən/: Bestätigung, Bescheinigung, Beweis

His good marks are an **attestation** to the skills of his teachers.

Seine guten Noten sind ein Beweis für die Fähigkeiten seiner Lehrer.

N.B. Die engl. Wörter *attest* und *attestation* werden im Vergleich zu den dt. *Attest* und *attestieren* recht selten gebraucht.

BANDAGE / BANDAGE

G *Bandage:* 1. Redewendung: siehe Beispiel
2. (Stützverband) (support) bandage
3. (Boxen) tape; (Turnen) wristband
4. (Pferdesport: Schutz für den Mittelfuß des Pferdes) bandage

1. Wenn es um Drogen geht, muß man **mit harten Bandagen / ohne Bandagen** kämpfen.

*When it's drugs we're dealing with, we have to fight **with no holds barred / with the gloves off**.*

E *bandage* /'bændɪdʒ/: 1. Verband (Im Gegensatz zu dt. Bandage ist das englische Wort ganz allgemein und bezeichnet nicht nur Stützverbände); Binde
2. Vgl. G4.

BANN, BANNEN / BAN

G *Bann:* 1. (starker Einfluß, Zauber) spell, charm, fascination
2. (geschichtlich) excommunication, Umschreibung mit 'excommunicated'

1. Die Frau zog ihn unwiderstehlich in ihren **Bann**.

*The woman cast an irresistible **spell** / exerted an irresistible **charm** over him.*

2. 1521 wurde der **Bann** über Luther ausgesprochen.

*Luther was **excommunicated** in 1521.*

G *bannen:* 1. to bewitch, captivate, entrance; (gebannt, auch) spellbound
(vgl. G. *Bann* 1)
2. to excommunicate (vgl. G *Bann* 2)
3. (Gefahr) to avert

1. Die schöne Musik **bannte** ihn förmlich.

   *The beautiful music positively **entranced** / **bewitched** him.*

   Wie **gebannt** starrte sie den Tiger an.

   *She stared at the tiger as if **spellbound**.*

3. Die Gefahr eines Atomkriegs schien vorerst **gebannt** zu sein.

   *The danger of a nuclear war seemed to have been **averted** for the time being.*

E *ban:* (n.) Verbot; (v.) verbieten

I don't think a **ban** on pornographic literature would achieve much.

*Ich glaube nicht, daß ein **Verbot** pornographischer Magazine viel erreichen würde.*

It won't be long before smoking is **banned** in restaurants.

*Es wird nicht lange dauern, bis das Rauchen in Restaurants **verboten** ist.*

BASIS / BASIS

G *Basis:* 1. (konkret: Sockel, mil. Stützpunkt usw.) base /beɪs/ (Pl. bases /'beɪsɪz/)
2. (abstrakt: Grundlage) basis /'beɪsɪs/ (Pl. bases /'beɪsiːz/)
3. (bei Parteien, Gewerkschaften usw.) the rank and file, the grass roots

1. Diese Säule hat im Gegensatz zu den anderen eine kreisförmige **Basis**.

   *Unlike the others, this column has a circular **base**.*

   Solche **Basen** für militärische Flugzeuge sind natürlich nicht gerade beliebt.

   *Such **bases** for military aircraft are of course not exactly popular.*

2. Dieser Vertrag bildet die **Basis** für den Ausbau der diplomatischen Beziehungen zwischen den beiden Ländern.

   *This treaty forms the **basis** for the extension of diplomatic relations between the two countries.*

3. Du bist schon zu lange im Parlament - du weißt nicht mehr, wie die **Basis** darüber denkt.

*You've been in Parliament too long - you no longer know what **the rank and file** think about it / what **the grass roots** feeling about it is.*

Ich weiß nicht, ob wir dieses Lohnabkommen der **Basis** verkaufen können.

*I don't know if we can get **the rank and file** / **the grass roots** (**membership**) to accept this wage agreement.*

E *basis* /ˈbeɪsɪs/: siehe G2.

BIEST / BEAST

G *Biest:* Die verschiedenen (abwertenden) Verwendungen des dt. Wortes decken sich nur selten mit dem engl. *beast.* Typische Übersetzungen:

(Kind) brat, little horror, (little) wretch
(Tier) damn(ed) animal
(Frau) bitch, cow
(Gegenstand) damn(ed) thing; Umschreibung mit 'damn(ed)' + adj., 'a hell of a' + noun, 'hellish' + adj.

Susanne ist ein kleines **Biest** - klaut dem eigenen Bruder die Schokolade.

*Susanne's a **little horror** - pinching her own brother's chocolate.*

Dieses **Biest** hat schon manche Ehe kaputtgemacht.

*That **bitch** has already wrecked a few marriages.*

Wenn dieses **Biest** noch einmal bellt, dann bringe ich es um.

*If that **damn(ed) animal** / **dog** barks again I'll kill it.*

Dieser Kühlschrank ist vielleicht ein **Biest** - ich kann ihn kaum bewegen.

*This fridge is **damn(ed) heavy** / **a hell of a weight** - I can scarcely move it.*

E *beast:* 1. (form.) Tier; *man and beast* = Mensch und Tier
2. (übertr.) Rohling, brutaler Mensch / Typ; Schuft
Das engl. Wort drückt meist Grausamkeit, Brutalität aus, wird aber manchmal auch scherzhaft verwendet.

1. The elephant is a noble **beast**.

*Der Elefant ist ein edles **Tier**.*

2. He used to hit her every day - what a **beast**!

*Jeden Tag hat er sie geschlagen - so ein **brutaler Mensch**!*

You **beast** - you've eaten my cake! *Du **Schuft** - du hast meinen Kuchen gegessen!*

BIGOTT / BIGOTED

G *bigott:* (übertrieben fromm) too/overly pious, too/overly devout (kein Einzelwortäquivalent im Engl.); (heuchlerisch) hypocritical, (in religiösen Kontexten) sanctimonious

E *bigoted* /ˈbɪgətɪd/: (engstirnig) intolerant (anderen Leuten gegenüber, die z.b. einer anderen Konfession oder Rasse angehören oder andere politische Ansichten haben)

It's pointless discussing politics with him - he's hopelessly **bigoted**.
*Es hat keinen Sinn, mit ihm über Politik zu diskutieren - er ist hoffnungslos **intolerant**.*

N.B. E *bigoted* is a much more commonly used word than *bigott* in German. The E noun *bigot* /ˈbɪgət/ is used for a person who is bigoted.

BLANK / BLANK

G *blank:* 1. (glänzend) shining, shiny
2. (nackt) bare, naked
3. (rein - Unsinn usw.) sheer, utter, complete
4. (pleite) broke, skint

1. Eine halbe Stunde scheuerte sie den Fußboden, bis er **blank** war.
*She scrubbed the floor for half an hour until it was **shining**.*

2. Es stört doch keinen, wenn so ein Kleinkind mit **blankem** Hintern am Strand herumtollt.
*Nobody minds a toddler like that romping about the beach with a **bare** bottom.*

3. Was du da erzählst, ist doch **blanker** Unsinn!
*What you're saying is **utter** nonsense!*

4. Ich würde dir liebend gern die Bluse kaufen, aber ich bin **blank**.
*I'd love to buy you the blouse, but I'm **broke**.*

E *blank:* 1. **leer, unausgefüllt;** *blank space* = **Lücke**
2. **verständnislos; Umschreibung mit** *Blackout* , *Mattscheibe*

1. You have to put a suitable word in the **blank** space.

   *Sie müssen ein passendes Wort in die **Lücke** einsetzen.*

   blank cheque
   blank form
   blank verse
   blank (cartridge)

   ***Blanko**scheck*
   ***Blanko**formular*
   ***Blank**vers*
   ***Platz**patrone*

2. He just gave me a **blank** look when I tried my Italian.

   *Er schaute mich nur **verständnislos** an, als ich es mit meinem Italienisch probierte.*

   My mind went **blank** when the examiner started asking questions.

   *Ich hatte einen **Blackout**, als der Prüfer begann, mir Fragen zu stellen.*

SECTION A - EXERCISES

A. *Translate the words in brackets so that they fit the sentences.*

1. My brother has just .... (absolvieren) a computer course.

2. I can't abide the thought of going on holiday with a little .... (Biest) like that!

3. My grandfather has got a very .... (akkurat) house.

4. That may well be the predominant opinion among you and the other managers, but it's not what the .... (Basis) think.

5. Luckily we don't have to rely on mains electricity in our holiday home - we've got our own .... (Aggregat).

6. His enormous success in San Francisco has ....(animieren) me to apply for a job there too.

7. The teenager stared at the pop star as if .... (gebannt).

8. He's so hopelessly.............................(engstirnig / intolerant) that it's pointless trying to discuss racial equality with him.

9. .... (Die Akteure) in the attempted coup have already been seized and dealt with.

10. Well, Tomkins, if you want to be excused from cross-country running, you'll have to bring me a(n)............................. (Attest) from your G.P.

11. If you have strained your thigh muscle, I think you'll need to rest it for a while - and make sure you wear a .... (Bandage) the next time you play.

12. All you have to do in this practice exercise is to fill in the .... (Lücken).

B. *Translate the following:*

1. *Er arbeitet im Akkord.*
2. *antike Möbel*
3. *ägyptische Altertümer*
4. *blanker Unsinn*
5. *eine Platzpatrone*
6. *eine akkurate Schrift*
7. *aus freien Stücken*
8. *das Bremsaggregat*

C. Match the words on the left with their definitions on the right. There are some items on the right that you won't need.

(a) antic
(b) blank (noun)
(c) basis
(d) antiquity
(e) aggregate
(f) animator
(g) antique
(h) to ban s.o.
(i) base

(1) s.o. who organises activities for children on holiday
(2) the starting-point, or fundamentals, for a discussion
(3) an old object, often collected for its beauty or value
(4) to cast a spell on s.o., as done by witches
(5) a harmless cartridge or bullet fired from a gun
(6) s.th. to rest a statue or ornament on
(7) shiny, reflecting light
(8) an absurd action or childish trick
(9) the sum total
(10) the far distant past
(11) an electricity generator
(12) s.o. who creates the illusion of movement, e.g. in a cartoon film
(13) to captivate or entrance s.o.
(14) a radical, left-wing political group
(15) to forbid or exclude s.o. from entering a place, e.g. a football ground or a disco

D. TRUE OR FALSE?

Mark the following statements true or false by writing T or F in the appropriate column. Write corrections for the false statements in the column on the right.

	T	F	CORRECTION
1. People who act in an affected way are said to put on airs and graces.			
2. Naughty children are often put under arrest by their parents.			
3. Catholics usually go to confession to be absolved from their sins.			
4. If no one forced her to do piece-work, then she did it of her own accord.			
5. A bigot is someone who is too pious or hypocritical.			
6. Clowns often perform antics.			

SECTION B

BLENDE / BLEND
BLENDEN / BLEND

G *Blende:* 1. (Foto., Opt.) aperture; oder 'f-Nummer' angeben; oder beides
2. (an Fenstern) blind
3. (Sonnenblende) sun visor (Auto); lens-hood (Fotoapparat)

1. Bei dieser Mittagssonne brauchst du **Blende** 16.	*You need an **aperture of f/16** in this midday sun.*

G *blenden:* (auch übertr.) to dazzle, blind

Die Sonne hat mich **geblendet**, und ich konnte nicht richtig aufschlagen.	*The sun **dazzled** me and I couldn't serve properly.*
Sie hat sich von diesen leeren Versprechungen **blenden** lassen.	*She has let herself be **dazzled** by these empty promises.*

E *blend:* (n.) Mischung; (v.) mischen

He always buys an especially strong **blend** of tea.	*Er kauft immer eine besonders kräftige **Teemischung**.*

BLUTIG / BLOODY

G *blutig:* bloody. Aber wegen der sehr häufigen Verwendung dieses Wortes als Kraftausdruck bieten Umschreibungen oft bessere Übersetzungsmöglichkeiten: siehe Beispiele.

Es war ein besonders **blutiger** Krieg.	*It was a particularly **bloody** war.*
Mein Gott! Dein Hemd ist ganz **blutig**!	*My God! Your shirt's **got blood** all over it!*
Ich werde dieses Schwein **blutig** schlagen!	*I'll beat that bastard **to a pulp**! / I'll beat **the hell out of** that bastard!*
ein **blutiger** Anfänger	*a **complete** / an **absolute** beginner*
Das ist mein **blutiger** Ernst.	*I'm **deadly** serious.*

E *bloody:* blutig (siehe oben). Aber auch ein sehr häufig zu hörender Kraftausdruck, der heutzutage nur wenige Leute schockiert.

Turn that **bloody** radio down! *Stell das **verdammte** / das **Scheiß**radio leiser.*

BRANCHE / BRANCH

G *Branche:* 1.(Geschäftszweig) trade, line of business
2.(Wirtschaftszweig) industry, sector
3.(Fachgebiet) field, area

1. Ich kann dir den Videorecorder etwas billiger besorgen: ich kenne nämlich jemanden aus der **Branche**.

   *I can get you the video recorder a bit cheaper: I know someone who works in the **trade**.*

   Popmusik? In dieser **Branche** kannst du dich auf nichts verlassen.

   *Pop music? You can't rely on anything in that **line of business**.*

2. Der Aufschwung in der Stahlindustrie ist nicht zu verkennen. Die gesamte **Branche** meldet neue Aufträge.

   *The upswing in the steel industry is unmistakeable. The whole **industry / sector** is reporting new orders.*

3. Herr Schmidt arbeitet in der gleichen **Branche** wie wir - er ist auch Sprachwissenschaftler.

   *Herr Schmidt works in the same **area/ field** as us - he's a linguist as well.*

E *branch:* 1.(Baum) Ast
2.(bei Firmen usw.) Filiale, Zweigstelle

1. We'll have to cut off the lower **branches** on that elm.

   *Wir müssen die unteren **Äste** von dieser Ulme absägen.*

2. I believe Woolworth's have closed several **branches** recently.

   *Ich glaube, Woolworth hat in letzter Zeit mehrere **Filialen** geschlossen.*

   Does your bank have a **branch** on the new estate?

   *Hat Ihre Bank eine **Zweigstelle** in der neuen Siedlung?*

CHOR / CHOIR, CHORE, CHORUS, CORE

G *Chor:* 1. (Gruppe von Personen, die gemeinsam singen; Teil einer Kirche) choir
          2. (gemeinsames Singen, Sprechen usw.; bei antiken Tragödien) chorus

1. Er ist seit Jahren Mitglied des Kirchen**chors**.
    He's been a member of the church **choir** *for years.*

2. "Auf Wiedersehen", rief die Gruppe im **Chor**.
    A **chorus** *of goodbyes came from the group.*

E *choir* /'kwaɪə/: siehe G1.

E *chore* /tʃɔː/: 1. Umschreibung mit *lästig*; lästige Arbeit / Pflicht
                2. (pl.) Hausarbeit

1. It's a **chore** having to write these school reports every six months.
    Es ist **lästig**, *jedes Halbjahr diese Zeugnisse schreiben zu müssen.*

2. My children do most of the (household) **chores**.
    Meine Kinder erledigen die meiste **Hausarbeit**.

E *chorus* /'kɔːrəs/: 1. Refrain
                    2. siehe G2.

1. I want you all to join in on the **chorus**.
    Ich möchte, daß ihr alle den **Refrain** *mitsingt.*

E *core* /kɔː/: Kern (eines Apfels, einer Sache, eines Reaktors, eines Problems)

a **choir** /'kwaɪə/   a **core** /kɔː/

CLIQUE / CLIQUE

G *Clique:* 1. (von Freunden usw.) crowd, bunch; Umschreibung mit *all her/their/the* usw.
2. (abwertend) clique

1. Es ist eine ganz nette **Clique** - wir treffen uns jeden Freitagabend in der Kneipe.
   *It's a really nice **crowd / bunch** - we meet in the pub every Friday evening.*

   Morgen hat Doris Geburtstag, und sie hat ihre ganze **Clique** eingeladen.
   *It's Doris's birthday tomorrow and she's invited **all her friends / her whole crowd**.*

2. Gegen eine so einflußreiche **Clique** sind wir hilflos.
   *We're helpless against such an influential **clique**.*

E *clique* /kliːk/: siehe G2. Das engl. Wort ist immer abwertend.

CRUX / CRUX

G *Crux:* (Problem, Schwierigkeit) problem, trouble, (bes. lästig) nuisance

Die **Crux** bei solchen Reisen ist, daß man nie allein sein kann.
*The **problem** with this sort of tour is that you can never be on your own. / It's a **nuisance** that on this sort of tour you can never be on your own.*

E *crux* /krʌks/: der Kern der Sache, der springende Punkt, die Hauptsache

Of course, that's the **crux** of the matter - who's going to provide the money?
*Das ist natürlich **der springende Punkt** - wer wird das Geld bereitstellen?*

DAMM / DAM

G *Damm:* 1. (zwischen Insel und Festland) causeway
2. (Ufer-, Bahn-, Straßendamm) embankment
3. (Deich) dyke
4. (Staudamm) dam
5. (anat.) perineum
6. (Idiom) *auf dem Damm:* OK, fit, in good shape, one's usual self

1. Wie lang ist der **Damm** zwischen Sylt und dem Festland?
   *How long is the **causeway** between Sylt and the mainland?*

5. Nach seiner **Damm**-Operation fühlte er sich viel besser.
   *After the operation on his **perineum**, he felt a lot better.*

6. Nach dem Urlaub war ich wieder auf dem **Damm**.
   *After my holiday I felt **OK** again / I was **my usual self** again.*

E *dam:* Staudamm, Talsperre

a **dam**   a **causeway**   a **dyke**

DEFINITIV / DEFINITIVE

G definitiv: 1.(sicher, eindeutig)   definite(ly), for sure
            2.(endgültig: Antwort, Entscheidung usw.) final, definitive

1. Wir wissen jetzt **definitiv**, daß diese Diagnose falsch war.
   *We now know **definitely / for sure** that this diagnosis was wrong.*

2. Nur das Verfassungsgericht kann die Sache **definitiv** entscheiden.
   *Only the Constitutional Court can make a **final / definitive** decision in the matter.*

E *definitive* /dɪ'fɪnətɪv/: 1. (bei Biographien, Chroniken, Ausgaben usw.) maßgeblich; Umschreibung (siehe unten). Das engl. Wort drückt aus, daß das Vorliegende so gut gelungen ist, daß es in absehbarer Zeit keiner Ergänzung, Änderung oder Korrektur bedürfen wird.

2. Vgl. G2.

1. This is the **definitive** biography of Churchill.
   *Dies ist die **maßgebliche** Churchill-Biographie.*

   This is the **definitive** collection of Rolling Stones tracks.
   *Eine bessere Sammlung von Rolling-Stones-Stücken **gibt es nicht**.*

DEKORATEUR(IN) / DECORATOR

G *Dekorateur(in):* (von Schaufenstern) window-dresser
(von Theater- und Filmkulissen: Bühnenbildner[in])
set designer
(von Innenräumen) interior designer / decorator

E *decorator:* Maler, im Sinne von jdm., der Innenräume tapeziert und streicht.

We've got the **decorators** in next week.
*Nächste Woche haben wir die **Maler** im Haus.*

Vgl. *interior decorator*, das einen Beruf mit künstlerischem Anspruch bezeichnet: Innenarchitekt(in), Raumgestalter(in), Dekorateur(in) (siehe oben).

a **window-dresser**   a **decorator**

DEKORATION / DECORATION

G *Dekoration:* 1. (Schaufenster) window-dressing
2. (Verzierung, Schmuck) decoration
3. (Bühnen-) set
4. (im Restaurant usw.) décor / ˈdeɪkɔː/

1. Auf eine gute **Dekoration** legt jedes
Kaufhaus großen Wert.

*Every store attaches great importance
to good **window-dressing**.*

2. Die **Dekoration** des Saals für das
Kostümfest war ein voller Erfolg.

*The **decoration** of the hall for the
fancy dress ball was a complete
success.*

3. Ich fand die **Bühnendekoration**
recht karg.

*I found the **set** very austere.*

4. Die **Dekoration** im neuen China-
Restaurant ist vollkommen übertrieben.

*The **décor** in the new Chinese
restaurant is way over the top.*

E *decoration:* vgl. G2

Christmas **decorations**   Weihnachts***schmuck***

DEKORIEREN / DECORATE

G *dekorieren:* 1. (Schaufenster) to dress
2. (schmücken) to decorate

1. Frau Schmidt ist gerade dabei, das
Hauptfenster zu **dekorieren**.

*Frau Schmidt is just **dressing** the
main window.*

E *decorate:* 1. schmücken, verzieren
2. (Zimmer) neu herrichten (d.h. tapezieren und / oder anstreichen)
3. (mil.) auszeichnen

1. The room was **decorated** with balloons
and streamers.

*Der Raum war mit Ballons und Papier-
schlangen **geschmückt**.*

2. We're having the dining-room **decorated** next week.
Wir lassen das Eßzimmer nächste Woche **neu herrichten.**

3. He was **decorated** with the Iron Cross.
Er wurde mit dem Eisernen Kreuz **ausgezeichnet.**

DELIKAT / DELICATE

G *delikat:* 1. (wohlschmeckend) delicious
2. (heikel, empfindlich) delicate, sensitive

1. Das Lammfleisch in diesem Restaurant war besonders **delikat.**
The lamb in this restaurant was particularly **delicious.**

2. Er verstand es, das **delikate** Problem diskret zu behandeln.
He knew how to deal with the **delicate / sensitive** problem discreetly.

E *delicate* /'delɪkət/: **fein, zart, empfindlich, anfällig; siehe auch G2.**

The tea service was made of a beautiful, **delicate** porcelain.
Das Teeservice war aus einem schönen, **zarten** Porzellan.

He was a pale boy of **delicate** health.
Er war ein blasser Junge von **anfälliger / zarter** Gesundheit.

DEMOLIEREN / DEMOLISH

G *demolieren:* **to smash up, to wreck, (Rowdys usw.) to vandalize**

Wenn seine Kinder auch kommen, werden sie unsere ganzen Möbel **demolieren.**
If his children come too, they'll **smash up / wreck** all our furniture.

Sein Porsche wurde von Rowdys **demoliert.**
His Porsche was **vandalized** by hooligans.

E *demolish* /dɪˈmɒlɪʃ/: 1. (Gebäude) abreißen
2. (Argumente usw.) zunichte machen
3. (ugs., Essen) vertilgen, verschlingen

1. That old brewery is being **demolished** after all.
   Diese alte Brauerei wird jetzt doch abgerissen.

2. She had soon **demolished** all his arguments.
   Bald hatte sie seine ganzen Argumente zunichte gemacht.

3. He was so hungry that he managed to **demolish** a whole chicken.
   Er war so hungrig, daß es ihm gelang, ein ganzes Huhn zu vertilgen / verschlingen.

a **vandalized** car   a **demolished** house

DEMONSTRATIV / DEMONSTRATIVE

G *demonstrativ:* 1. (auffallend-provozierend) ostentatious(ly), pointed(ly), Umschreibung mit *to make a point of*
2. (deutlich) clear, etc.
3. (gramm.) demonstrative /dɪˈmɒnstrətɪv/

1. Als der Palästinenser aufstand, verließ der israelische Botschafter **demonstrativ** den Saal.
   *When the Palestinian stood up, the Israeli ambassador **pointedly** left the room.*

   Demonstrativ bezeichnete er Schlesien als einen Teil Deutschlands.
   *He **made a point of** referring to Silesia as a part of Germany.*

2. Sie weigerte sich **demonstrativ**, ihm die Hand zu geben.
   *She **ostentatiously** refused to shake hands with him.*

Dies ist ein **demonstratives** Beispiel für seine Unfähigkeit, Kompromisse zu schließen.

*This is a **clear** example of his inability to make compromises.*

3. 'That' gehört zu den **Demonstrativ**pronomina im Englischen.

*'That' is one of the **demonstrative** pronouns in English.*

E *demonstrative* /dɪ'mɒnstrətɪv/: 1. (Charaktereigenschaft) gefühlsbetont
2. siehe G3.

She was a very **demonstrative** girl, given to both tears and laughter.

*Sie war ein sehr **gefühlsbetontes** Mädchen, das sowohl zum Weinen als auch zum Lachen neigte.*

DIFFERENZIERT / DIFFERENTIATED

G *differenziert* / E *differentiated* /ˌdɪfə'renʃieɪtɪd/: Während das dt. *differenziert* auch als Adjektiv benutzt wird, existiert die engl. Form *differentiated* praktisch nur als echtes Partizip. Insofern kann behauptet werden, daß das adjektivierte *differenziert* so gut wie nie durch *differentiated* allein übersetzt werden kann, obwohl sich die Hinzufügung geeigneter Adverbien (wie bei *subtly / cleverly differentiated* - vgl. Beispiele unten) in manchen Kontexten anbietet. Die Übersetzung bleibt schwierig und stark kontextgebunden.

1. (den verschiedenen Aspekten, Nuancen und feinen Unterschieden einer Sache, eines Problems Rechnung tragend) deep, precise, perceptive, detailed

2. (anspruchsvoll, einen verfeinerten Geschmack vorweisend) sophisticated, discriminating

3. (verschiedenartig) varied, diverse

1. Faktisch stimmt alles in Ihrem Bericht, aber Ihre Analyse der Fakten ist nicht sehr **differenziert**.

*Factually, everything is correct in your report, but your analysis of the facts is not very **deep/precise/perceptive**.*

2. Seinen **differenzierten** Geschmack in der klassischen Musik bezeugte seine CD-Sammlung.

*His collection of CDs testified to his **sophisticated/discriminating** taste in classical music.*

3. Die äußerst **differenzierte** Sprache dieses Essayisten ist kaum nachzuahmen.

*The extremely **subtly differentiated/ extremely varied** language of this essayist can hardly be imitated.*

DISPONIEREN / DISPOSE OF

G *disponieren:* (Vorbereitungen usw. treffen) to make arrangements/ plans

Wir können erst dann **disponieren**, wenn der genaue Zinssatz festgelegt wird.

*We can't **make arrangements** until the exact interest rate is fixed.*

E *dispose of:* loswerden, beseitigen

We now had a new washing-machine, but how were we supposed to **dispose of** the old one?

*Wir hatten jetzt eine neue Waschmaschine, aber wie sollten wir die alte **loswerden**?*

DOUBLE / DOUBLE

G *Double:* (Film) stand-in

Du bist wohl verrückt, einen solchen Stunt ohne **Double** machen zu wollen.

*You must be crazy, wanting to do a stunt like that without a **stand-in**.*

E *double:* 1. Doppelgänger(in)
2. (Tennis, meist im Pl.) Doppel
3. Doppelzimmer (Kurzform für *double room*)
4. (bei Mengen, Getränken usw.) Doppelte
5. (Idiom) *at the double* = sofort, schnellstens

1. Do you know you've got a **double**?

   *Wissen Sie, daß Sie einen **Doppelgänger** haben?*

2. Who won the ladies' **doubles**?

   *Wer hat das Damen**doppel** gewonnen?*

3. They haven't got any more **doubles**.

   *Sie haben keine **Doppelzimmer** mehr.*

4. When he's drinking whisky, he only orders **doubles**.

   *Wenn er Whisky trinkt, bestellt er nur **Doppelte**.*

DRACHE, DRACHEN / DRAGON

G *Drache(n):*   1. (aus Papier, für Kinder usw.) kite
                     2. (Fluggerät für Drachenflieger) hang-glider
                     3. (zänkische Frau) dragon, battleaxe
                     4. (furchterregendes Tier aus Sage usw.) dragon

1. Hier darfst du deinen **Drachen** nicht steigen lassen - siehst du die Hochspannungsleitungen nicht?

   *You can't fly your **kite** here - can't you see the overhead power lines?*

2. Wieso hat er sich einen **Drachen** gekauft, wenn er an Höhenangst leidet?

   *Why has he bought a **hang-glider** * if he suffers from fear of heights?*

3. Seine neue Sekretärin ist ein richtiger **Drachen**.

   *His new secretary is a real **dragon / battleaxe**.*

4. St. Georg hat den **Drachen** erschlagen.

   *St. George slew the **dragon**.*

* N.B. **Hang-glider** = (1) Drachen; (2) Drachenflieger - Siehe auch **DRACHENFLIEGER / DRAGONFLY**, Seite 157.

E *dragon:*   siehe G3 und G4.

a **dragon**   a(n) (old) **dragon**   a **kite**

EBBE / EBB

G *Ebbe:* 1.(Wechsel von Hochwasser zu Niedrigwasser) Umschreibung mit *the tide is going out;* (meist in bezug auf Schiffahrt) ebb tide

          2. (Zustand des erreichten Niedrigwassers) low tide; Umschreibung mit *the tide is out.*

          3. (übertr.) Umschreibung, manchmal mit *at a low ebb*

1. Es ist **Ebbe**: es hat keinen Sinn, hier zu baden.

   The tide's going out - there's no point going for a swim here.

   Wir können erst mit der **Ebbe** auslaufen.

   *We shall have to wait for the **ebb tide** to sail.*

   Ebbe und Flut

   the tides

2. Bei **Ebbe** kann man hier sehr schöne Muscheln finden.

   *You can find very nice shells here **at low tide** / **when the tide's out**.*

3. Im Staatssäckel herrscht **Ebbe**.

   *The national coffers **are empty**.*

   In seinem Geldbeutel herrscht immer **Ebbe**.

   *He's always **hard up/short of cash**./ His finances are always **at a low ebb**.*

E *ebb:* siehe G1 - 3. Das Nomen *ebb* tritt meistens in den Verbindungen *ebb tide* und *at a low ebb / reach a low ebb* auf. Letztere wird fast immer im übertragenen Sinn verwendet und bezieht sich meist auf den Gemütszustand eines Menschen oder auf zwischenmenschliche Beziehungen: siehe Beispiele.

Ever since he broke up with Sandra he's been **at a** pretty **low ebb**.

*Seitdem er mit Sandra Schluß gemacht hat, fühlt er sich ziemlich **elend**.*

Relations between the two countries reached **a low ebb** in 1972.

*Die Beziehungen zwischen den beiden Ländern gelangten 1972 auf einen **Tiefpunkt**.*

SECTION B - EXERCISES

A . SYNONYMS - Match the words on the left with their synonyms on the right.

1. CHORE	goes with	F-NUMBER	DELICIOUS
2. DISPOSE OF	goes with	AT LOW TIDE	CHOIR
3. FIELD	goes with	SENSITIVE	PAINTER
4. DEMOLISH	goes with	MIXTURE	DAZZLE
5. BLEND	goes with	CORE	GET RID OF
6. AT A LOW EBB	goes with	REFRAIN	VANDALIZE
7. CHORUS	goes with	PULL DOWN	SMASH UP
8. DECORATOR	goes with	DEPRESSED	
9. APERTURE	goes with	BORING, ROUTINE TASK	
10. DELICATE	goes with	LINE OF BUSINESS	
		HAVE AVAILABLE	
		OPENING TIMES	

B . Translate the words in brackets so that they fit into the sentences.

1. In disputes like that, you have to fight......................... (mit harten Bandagen).

2. At the moment you can walk over to the island, but three hours from now the .... (Damm) will be completely covered by the incoming tide.

3. Of course the .... (Crux) at such conferences is that you are forced to be polite to people you don't like.

4. Do you think you could spare me half an hour to show me the ropes? I'm a(n) .... (blutiger Anfänger) here.

5. That actress is so racially prejudiced that she refused to do the kissing scene with the black man. They had to shoot it from a distance and use a .... (Double).

6. He slammed the door .... (demonstrativ) and left the room.

7. There's a really great atmosphere in "The Hedgehog's Revenge" every Friday night. Ann brings her whole .... (Clique) along and we have a super time.

8. This firm of solicitors has a definite policy of only recruiting ....(Akademiker).

9. Dr. Soredom has now .... (attestieren) that Fred is unable to continue in his present job.

C. ALL ABOUT 'DRACHEN'

Find the best translations of 'Drache(n)' (or one of its compounds) to put into the following sentences.

1. I never liked my old physics teacher much - she was a bit of an old ....

2. Little four-year-old Sebastian loves nothing more than to fly his .... from a hilltop on a windy day.

3. Frightening-looking ...., with red eyes and breathing fire, feature prominently in books of fairy tales.

4. I've got to buy a new .... The last one was irreparably damaged when I plummeted from the sky and hit the cliffs at Dover!

5. Mary's a runner, Tom's a skier, and Dan's an accomplished .... (Drachenflieger).

D. ALL ABOUT 'DEKORATION'

Find the best translations of 'Dekoration' (or one of its compounds) in the following sentences.

1. I thought the .... (Bühnendekoration) for 'A Day in the Death of Joe Egg' was outstanding.

2. What do you think of the .... in the new Indian restaurant?

3. I hardly ever buy anything at Rigby's, but I'm always tempted into the shop by the quality of the ....

4. I'll see to the invitations and Bill will take care of the music, but the .... of the room is your responsibility.

E. Translate the following phrases and sentences:

1. *eine kräftige Teemischung*
2. *Er sprach ihn von seinen Sünden frei.*
3. *Es ist Ebbe - bald ist das Meer 500 Meter weit weg.*
4. *die antike Baukunst*
5. *Er ist heute nicht auf dem Damm.*
6. *der Kern des Problems*
7. *Sie gab uns eine definitive Absage.*
8. *Der Fußboden war blank.*

SECTION C

ENORM / ENORMOUS

G *enorm* / E *enormous*: In den meisten Fällen entspricht das dt. *enorm* dem engl. *enormous* (wobei andere Übersetzungen wie *huge, vast, tremendous* stilistisch manchmal besser sind), nicht aber im umgangssprachlichen Sinn von *toll, fantastisch* usw.

8000 Mark im Monat - das ist ja **enorm**!   *8000 marks a month - that's **great / fantastic/incredible/marvellous**!*

EXEMPLARISCH / EXEMPLARY

G *exemplarisch:* wird am besten mit einer Umschreibung mit dem Nomen *example* übersetzt, weil das engl. *exemplary* meistens ein Werturteil beinhaltet.

Exemplarisches Lernen ist der Grundpfeiler seiner pädagogischen Theorie.
*Learning **by example** is the keystone of his educational theory.*

War das gerecht, den Deserteur **exemplarisch** zu bestrafen?
*Was it just to punish the deserter as an **example** to the other soldiers?*

Die Tabellen sind rein **exemplarischer** Natur und keineswegs vollständig.
*The tables are merely meant to provide **examples** and are by no means complete.*

E *exemplary* /ɪgˈzemplərɪ/:   **mustergültig, beispielhaft, vorbildlich** (mit positivem Werturteil)

His behaviour throughout the crisis was quite **exemplary**.
*Sein Verhalten während der Krise war ganz **vorbildlich**.*

John has proved to be an **exemplary** pupil.
*John hat sich als **mustergültiger** Schüler erwiesen.*

EXERZIEREN/ EXERCISE

G *exerzieren:* 1. (mil.) to drill
2. (erproben) to practise

1. Wie lange wollen Sie diese armen Rekruten noch **exerzieren** lassen?
   How much longer do you want to drill these poor recruits?

2. Diese Methode der Einschüchterung haben sie schon einmal durch**exerziert**.
   *They have already **practised** this method of intimidation.*

E *exercise:* 1. sich bewegen (um fit zu werden usw.)
2. (Hund usw.) ausführen, spazierenführen
3. (Recht, Macht usw.) ausüben, Gebrauch machen von
4. (mil.) ins Manöver gehen

1. If you **exercised** a bit more you might be out of breath less often.
   *Wenn du **dich** etwas mehr **bewegen** würdest, wärst du vielleicht weniger oft außer Atem.*

2. How often do you have to **exercise** a dog like this?
   *Wie oft muß man einen solchen Hund **ausführen** / **spazierenführen**?*

3. The judge **exercised** his right to adjourn the proceedings.
   *Der Richter **machte** von seinem Recht **Gebrauch**, die Gerichtsverhandlung zu vertagen.*

4. The troops will be **exercising** in Norway next month.
   *Die Truppen **gehen** nächsten Monat in Norwegen **ins Manöver**.*

EXHIBITIONIST(IN) / EXHIBITIONIST

G *Exhibitionist(in)* / E *exhibitionist:* Sowohl das deutsche wie auch das englische Wort können zwei Bedeutungen haben:

1. Jmd. mit einer sexualpsychologischen Störung, der den krankhaften Zwang spürt, seine Geschlechtsteile in der Öffentlichkeit zu entblößen;

2. Jmd., der in weniger drastischer Weise versucht (z.B. durch extravagante Kleidung oder übertriebenes Benehmen), die Aufmerksamkeit anderer auf sich zu lenken.

Im dt. Wort überwiegt weitaus die *erste*, im engl. Wort die *zweite* Bedeutung. Das engl. Wort hat also recht selten eine sexuelle Bedeutung.

G *Exhibitionist(in):* (sex.) flasher; (selten) exhibitionist
E *exhibitionist* /ˌeksɪˈbɪʃənɪst/: Umschreibung mit *im Mittelpunkt stehen* usw.; (selten) Exhibitionist(in)

Angeblich sind **Exhibitionisten** meist nicht aggressiv.	*Apparently **flashers** are not normally aggressive.*
John's such an **exhibitionist**: at our last party he dressed up as the Queen - with a crown, flippers and a diver's mask!	*John hat ein übertriebenes Bedürfnis, im Mittelpunkt zu stehen: Auf unserer letzten Party hat er sich als die Königin verkleidet - mit Krone, Flossen und Tauchermaske!*

a **flasher**　　　　an **exhibitionist**

EXISTENZ / EXISTENCE

G *Existenz:* 1. (Dasein, Vorhandensein) existence
　　　　　　　2. (Lebensgrundlage) livelihood, living, life, secure job
　　　　　　　3. (abwertend: Mensch) *verkrachte Existenz* = failure

1. An der **Existenz** dieser Lager zweifelt keiner mehr. — *Nobody doubts the **existence** of these camps any longer.*

2. Dieses Handelsembargo wird für viele Menschen den Verlust ihrer **Existenz** bedeuten. — *For many people this trade embargo will mean the loss of their **livelihood**.*

   Während der Rezession fristete sie eine kümmerliche **Existenz** als Putzfrau. — *During the recession she eked out a miserable **living** as a cleaner.*

   Als Beamter hat er eine vollkommen gesicherte **Existenz**. — *As a civil servant he has a completely **secure livelihood / job** (he has complete **job security**).*

Er wanderte nach Neuseeland aus, um sich eine neue **Existenz** aufzubauen.
He emigrated to New Zealand to make a new life for himself.

das **Existenzminimum**
subsistence level

E *existence:* siehe *nur* **G1.**

EXKURSION / EXCURSION

G *Exkursion:* field trip, study trip

Exkursionen stellen einen wesentlichen Teil eines Geologiestudiums dar.
Field trips / Study trips constitute an essential part of a geology course.

E *excursion* /ɪkˈskɜːʃn/: **Ausflug, (auch übertr.) Abstecher**

Our club had arranged a day **excursion** to the seaside.
Unser Klub hatte einen Tagesausflug an die Küste arrangiert.

After a short **excursion** into politics, he returned to writing.
Nach einem kurzen Abstecher in die Politik wandte er sich wieder dem Schreiben zu.

EXPEDITION / EXPEDITION

G *Expedition:* 1. (Versandabteilung) dispatch office / department
2. (für Forschungszwecke usw.) expedition

1. Herr Jonas arbeitet in der **Expeditionsabteilung** unseres Versandhauses.
   Herr Jonas works in the dispatch department of our mail order firm.

2. Er verschwand während einer **Expedition** zum Amazonas-Dschungel.
   He disappeared during an expedition to the Amazon Jungle.

E *expedition* /ˌekspəˈdɪʃn/: siehe **G2.**

EXPOSÉ / EXPOSÉ

G *Exposé:* 1. (Bericht, Kurzmitteilung) report, memorandum
2. (für Film, Buch usw.) draft, scenario, outline

1. Der Ministerialbeamte legte seine Meinung in einem dreiseitigen **Exposé** nieder.

   *The ministry official set down his opinion in a three-page **report** / **memorandum**.*

2. Das **Exposé** für die erste Folge der Fernsehserie wurde angenommen.

   *The **draft** / **scenario** / **outline** for the first episode of the TV series was accepted.*

E *exposé* /ekˈspəʊzeɪ/: Enthüllung, Enthüllungsreportage, Aufdeckung (von etwas Skandalösem)

This week's Sunday Smear contains a juicy **exposé** of sex orgies among people in high places.

*Die Sunday Smear enthält diese Woche eine deftige **Enthüllungsreportage** über Sexorgien unter Leuten in hohen Positionen.*

EXTRAVAGANT / EXTRAVAGANT

G *extravagant:* 1. (Kleidung usw.) flamboyant, outlandish, (weniger oft) extravagant (aber vgl. E *extravagant*)
2. (Persönlichkeit) eccentric, unusual

1. Solange ich sie kenne, kleidet sie sich so **extravagant**.

   *As long as I've known her, she's dressed as **flamboyantly** / **outlandishly** / **extravagantly** as this.*

   Ich finde dieses Tapetenmuster ziemlich **extravagant**.

   *I think this wallpaper pattern is rather **flamboyant** / **outlandish**.*

2. Sie war eine **extravagante** Frau, die einem nach einer gewissen Zeit auf die Nerven ging.

   *She was an **eccentric** / **unusual** woman, who got on one's nerves after a certain time.*

E *extravagant* /ɪk'strævəgənt/: kann sich wie das dt. *extravagant* auf einen ausgefallenen und auffallenden Stil beziehen, bedeutet aber viel öfter *zu teuer, verschwenderisch*. In manchen Fällen ist das Wort im Engl. zweideutig: *an extravagant dress* würde normalerweise als *ein zu teures Kleid* verstanden werden, könnte aber theoretisch *ein Kleid mit extravagantem Muster* bezeichnen.

I always feel it's **extravagant** to drink wine in this sort of restaurant.	*Ich habe immer das Gefühl, daß es zu teuer ist, Wein in einem solchen Restaurant zu trinken.*
For an **extravagant** woman like her, housekeeping money had no significance.	*Für eine verschwenderische Frau wie sie hatte Haushaltsgeld keine Bedeutung.*

FATAL / FATAL

G *fatal:* 1. (peinlich) embarrassing, awkward, painful
2. (verhängnisvoll, folgenschwer) fatal, dire, disastrous

1. Es war natürlich ein **fataler** Augenblick, als er sich nach ihrem Baby erkundigte, das im vorigen Monat gestorben war.

   *It was of course an **embarrassing / painful** moment when he asked after her baby, who had died the previous month.*

2. Dieses Mißverständnis zwischen den beiden Botschaftern sollte **fatale** Folgen haben.

   *This misunderstanding between the two ambassadors was to have **fatal / dire** consequences.*

E *fatal:* 1. tödlich
2. siehe G2.

1. A single bite from this snake can be **fatal**.   *Ein einziger Biß dieser Schlange kann tödlich sein.*

FETE / FETE

G *Fete:* party

Bei Udo gab es am Samstag wieder eine tolle **Fete**.   *There was another great **party** at Udo's place on Saturday.*

E *fete* (auch: *fête*) /feɪt/: kein genaues dt. Äquivalent. Das Wort bezeichnet mehrere Arten von Fest, die meist im Freien stattfinden und dem Sammeln von Geld für karitative Zwecke dienen. Sie bieten dem Besucher verschiedene Spiele und Wettbewerbe als Unterhaltung, sowie (oft hausgemachte) Erfrischungen an. Besonders häufig sind folgende Zusammensetzungen; die angegebenen Übersetzungen sind nur approximativ:

charity **fete**	*Wohltätigkeitsbasar*
church **fete**	*Kirchenbasar*
village **fete**	*Dorffest*

FEUDAL / FEUDAL

G *feudal:* 1. (ugs., vornehm) fancy, posh
            2. (hist.) feudal

1. In einem so **feudalen** Restaurant war ich noch nie.   *I've never been to such a **fancy** / **posh** restaurant before.*

2. der **Feudal**staat   *the **feudal** state*

E *feudal* /'fju:də l/: *nur* G2.

FIEBER / FEVER

G *Fieber* / E *fever:* manchmal äquivalent (bes. bei Krankheitsnamen), aber das engl. *temperature* wird sehr oft bevorzugt.

(hohes) **Fieber** haben	*to have a (high) **temperature***
jemandem das **Fieber** messen	*to take s.o.'s **temperature***
Sie hat 39,5 **Fieber**.	*She's got a **temperature** of 39.5.*

Drüsen**fieber**	*glandular **fever***
Gelb**fieber**	*yellow **fever***
Heuschnupfen	*hay **fever***
Lampen**fieber**	*stage **fright***
Scharlach(**fieber**)	*scarlet **fever***

FIGUR / FIGURE

G *Figur:* 1. physique /fɪˈziːk/ (bes. von Männern, in bezug auf Muskulatur usw.); figure (von Frauen)
2. (ugs.: Person) character, bloke, (bes. AmE) guy
3. (Galionsfigur) figurehead
4. (sonst meist) figure

1. Nach sechs Wochen Bodybuilding müßte ich eine **Figur** haben, die sich sehen lassen kann, dachte er.

   After six weeks of bodybuilding I should have a pretty respectable physique, he thought.

   Uta hatte schon immer eine tolle **Figur**.

   Uta's always had a great figure.

2. Wer waren diese komischen **Figuren** vorhin?

   Who were those strange characters / blokes / guys just now?

3. In diesem Staat fungiert der Präsident nur als **Galionsfigur**.

   The President only functions as a figurehead in this state.

E *figure* /ˈfɪɡə/: 1. Zahl, Ziffer
2. (pl.) Rechnen
3. siehe G1 und G4.

1. On the side of the burnt-out plane the **figure** 7 could just be made out.

   Auf der Seite des ausgebrannten Flugzeugs konnte man die Zahl / Ziffer 7 gerade noch erkennen.

2. It's no good asking me - you know I'm hopeless at **figures**.

   Es hat keinen Zweck, mich zu fragen - du weißt doch, daß ich im Rechnen ein hoffnungsloser Fall bin.

FLAIR / FLAIR

G *Flair:* atmosphere, feel; (bei Personen auch) aura

Wer vermag schon, das besondere **Flair** von Paris zu beschreiben?

Who can describe the peculiar feel / atmosphere of Paris?

Er hatte das **Flair** eines Weltmannes.

He had the aura of a man of the world.

E *flair:* 1. Talent, Begabung, Umschreibung mit *begabt*
2. Gespür, Nase
3. Stil, Format

1. He's always had a **flair** for languages.
   *Er war schon immer sprach**begabt**.*

   His **flair** for football was discovered when he was at primary school.
   *Sein **Talent** für Fußball wurde schon in der Grundschule entdeckt.*

2. He has a **flair** for bargains.
   *Er hat ein **Gespür** für gute Geschäfte.*

3. I don't know if you can call her beautiful, but she's got **flair**.
   *Ich weiß nicht, ob man sie als schön bezeichnen kann, aber sie hat **Stil**.*

FORMAT / FORMAT

G *Format:* 1. (Rang, Niveau usw.) quality, class; (Zustand des Angesehenwerdens, Bekanntseins) stature; Format haben (ugs.) = to have class

2. (Größe usw.) format

1. Wir haben keine Hotels von internationalem **Format**.
   *We have no hotels of international **quality / class**.*

   In ihm haben wir einen Forscher von internationalem **Format**.
   *In him we have a researcher of international **stature**.*

   Man merkt ihm seine aristokratische Herkunft an - er hat **Format**.
   *You can tell he's descended from the aristocracy - he's got **class**.*

2. DIN-A4-**Format**
   *A4 **format***

E *format* /'fɔːmæt/: 1. 'Aufmachung' (einer Zeitschrift, Sendung usw.) in bezug auf Inhalt, Präsentation usw.
2. siehe G2.

1. We've got to change the **format** of the programme - otherwise we soon won't have any listeners left.
   *Wir müssen **Aufbau und Inhalt** der Sendung ändern - sonst haben wir bald keine Zuhörer mehr.*

FRANKIEREN / FRANK

G *frankieren:* Die Übersetzung hängt von der Art der Freimachung ab:

    1. (mit Briefmarke) to stamp, to put a stamp on;
    2. (mit Frankiermaschine) to frank

Der Brief war nicht einmal **frankiert**.

*There wasn't even a **stamp** on the letter. / The letter hadn't even been **franked**.*

E *frank:* 1. (Briefmarke) abstempeln
         2. siehe G2.

The stamp wasn't **franked**, and he steamed it off so that he could use it again.

*Die Briefmarke war nicht **abgestempelt**, und er löste sie über Dampf ab, um sie wiederzuverwenden.*

FREQUENZ / FREQUENCY

G *Frequenz:* 1. (bei Statistiken, Zahlen usw.) number, ratio oder Umschreibung
           2. (med.) Pulsfrequenz = pulse (rate)
           3. (tech.: Radiowellen usw.) frequency

1. Bestimmte Sprachkurse mußten wegen niedriger **Frequenzen** gestrichen werden.

*Certain language courses had to be cancelled because of low **numbers** (of participants).*

Bildungsminister und Eltern haben oft verschiedene Meinungen, was **Klassenfrequenzen** betrifft.

*Ministers of Education and parents often have differing views as far as **class sizes / staff-pupil ratios** are concerned.*

E *frequency* /'friːkwənsi/: 1. Häufigkeit
                       2. siehe G3.

FRIVOL / FRIVOLOUS

G *frivol:* 1. (schlüpfrig) dirty, smutty, indecent, (schwächer) risqué
        2. (leichtfertig) frivolous

1. Onkel Hans war für seine Vorliebe für **frivole** Geschichten bekannt.

*Uncle Hans was well-known for his partiality to **smutty / dirty** stories.*

E *frivolous* /ˈfrɪvələs/: Bezeichnet einen der Situation unangemessenen Mangel an Ernst: leichtfertig - aber Umschreibungen sind oft präziser.

Don't be frivolous - this is a serious matter.

Nimm es nicht auf die leichte Schulter - das ist eine ernste Angelegenheit.

His **frivolous** comments simply made everyone angry.

Seine lässig dahingeworfenen Bemerkungen verärgerten alle nur.

FRONTAL, FRONTAL- / FRONTAL

G *frontal, Frontal-:* läßt sich oft mit *frontal* übersetzen, aber:

Der Wagen prallte **frontal** mit dem Lkw zusammen.

The car collided with the lorry **head-on**.

Frontalzusammenstoß

head-on *collision*

Frontalunterricht

teacher-centred *teaching,* (*ugs.*) **chalk and talk**

E *frontal* /ˈfrʌntəl/: 1. (Blick, Foto, Darstellung usw.) von vorne, Frontal-, frontal; (med.) frontal
2. full frontal (nudity) = frontale Nacktdarstellung

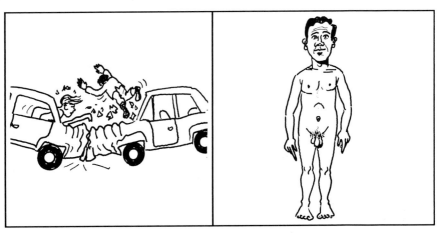

a **head-on** collision   **full-frontal** nudity

SECTION C - EXERCISES

A. SIMON SKROATEM'S SORDID SEXUAL SECRETS

Choose appropriate words from the following list to complete the story below. Do not use any word more than once. There are some words in the list which you will not need.

atmosphere	embarrassing	fatal	flasher	livelihood
class	exhibitionist	feast	format	numbers
detailed	existence	fête	frequency	party
differentiated	expedition	feudal	frivolous	physique
dirty	exposé	figure	frontal	posh
dispatch	exposure	flair	full-frontal	

To be honest I was deeply shocked when the truth came out. Simon Skroatem was a man I had looked up to for nearly 20 years. Manager of the (1) .... department of a huge banana company located just outside our village, he was also treasurer of the golf club, an active campaigner for Amnesty International, and the leading organiser for the village (2) .... in summer, held in the park next to the church, which raised money for the local orphanage. Also, thanks to regular visits to the fitness centre, he had an impressive (3) ....

At weekends he was usually to be seen in one of the many (4) .... restaurants in our area - he particularly liked the ones with real silver cutlery and solid brass candlesticks. But he wasn't a snob; far from it. If he heard that any local organisation, like the youth club, had run into difficulty because of falling (5) ...., he was the first one to go and try to help recruit new members. His enviable sense of humour meant that he was constantly in demand as an after-dinner speaker. Whenever Nelly Lovett, Director of the old people's home, wanted someone to entertain the old folks she would always try and get hold of Skroatem. Here was a man who loved both his fellow humans and a touch of luxury. He was well dressed, widely read, and sophisticated. In short, he had (6) ....

Things started going badly wrong when Lord Loopy spotted Skroatem coming out of a strip club in nearby Humpton. (What Loopy was doing in the area has never been satisfactorily explained.) It was, of course, a(n) (7) .... moment for Skroatem, who is said to have gone a deep shade of purple. Later, he confessed that he had always found the special (8) .... of this seedy part of Humpton irresistible, but it was to prove his undoing. A month later, a mistress at our local primary school saw him drunk in a Humpton pub, telling the sort of (9).................. jokes that even made her blush. That was a(n) (10) .... mistake, for among the listeners that night was Joe Sniffit, gossip columnist for the Humpton Chronicle. He then shadowed Skroatem for three months before publishing a(n) (11) .... report on Simon's Jekyll-and-Hyde lifestyle. This damning (12) .... unmasked Skroatem as being none other than the Humpton (13) ...., sought by the police for exposing himself on Humpton Common. Sniffit even claimed to have a(n) (14) .... photo of Skroatem caught in the act, though the Chronicle didn't dare to publish it. In any case, the police were then easily able to identify Simon, and the game was up. The scandal meant the loss of Simon's (15) .... , and the last I heard he was doing voluntary work in London's East End.

B. Mark the following statements true or false by writing T or F in the appropriate column. Write corrections for the false statements in the column on the right.

	T	F	CORRECTION
1. It's extravagant to eat in an expensive restaurant three times in one day.			
2. Film directors have to read through many exposés before deciding which films are worth making.			
3. After buying stamps at the post-office, you frank your letters.			
4. Pupils whose conduct is exemplary are usually liked by their teachers.			
5. Coaches sometimes take 50 old people on a day excursion to the seaside.			
6. Army recruits are often exercised on the parade ground.			
7. Political dissidents are sometimes kept under house arrest in repressive countries.			
8. One of the duties of a doctor is to attest that certain people are medically unfit for work.			

C. Translate the following:

1. *Du hast die Stelle bekommen? Das ist ja enorm!*
2. *Heuschnupfen*
3. *Drüsenfieber*
4. *jemandem das Fieber messen*
5. *Das ist mein blutiger Ernst.*
6. *der Damm bei Wilhelmshaven*
7. *die Akteure der Flugzeugentführung*
8. *Dieses Biest hat mir den Mann geklaut.*
9. *Such doch keine Stelle in der Bergbauindustrie: mit der ganzen Branche geht's bergab.*
10. *eine sehr akkurate Wohnung*
11. *ein delikates Problem*
12. *eine lästige Pflicht im Haushalt*

SECTION D

GOLF / GOLF

G *Golf:* 1. (der Golf - geog.) g<u>u</u>lf, bay
2. (das Golfspiel) golf

1. der (Persische) Golf
die **Golf**staaten
der **Golf** von Mexiko
der **Golf** von Neapel
der **Golf** von Biskaya

the (Persian) **Gulf**
the **Gulf** *states*
the **Gulf** *of Mexico*
the **Bay** *of Naples*
the **Bay** *of Biscay*

2. **Golf** spielen

to play **golf**

E *golf:* siehe *nur* G2.

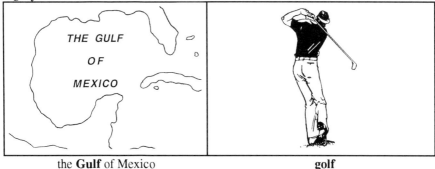

the **Gulf** of Mexico   golf

GRANDIOS / GRANDIOSE

G *grandios:* (ist im Gegensatz zum engl. *grandiose* meist positiv)
grand, tremendous, splendid, magnificent

Anläßlich des Besuchs des chinesischen Außenministers findet ein **grandioses** Sportfest statt.

A **grand** *sports festival is taking place on the occasion of the Chinese Foreign Minister's visit.*

Unseren Augen bot sich ein **grandioser** Anblick.

A **magnificent** *view met our eyes.*

E *grandiose* / 'grændi,əʊs/: (meist abwertend - zu groß, teuer usw.)
bombastisch, hochtrabend, größenwahnsinnig

These **grandiose** buildings seem to have been built to intimidate visitors.	*Diese **bombastischen** Gebäude sind anscheinend gebaut worden, um Besucher einzuschüchtern.*
I'm tired of his **grandiose** schemes - we need a more realistic approach.	*Ich habe seine **größenwahnsinnigen** Pläne satt - wir brauchen einen realistischeren Ansatz.*
A lot of **grandiose** rhetoric and nothing else.	*Eine Menge **hochtrabender** Rhetorik und sonst nichts.*

GRAZIÖS / GRACIOUS

G *graziös:* graceful

Er ist zwar klein und dick, aber er tanzt erstaunlich **graziös**.	*Although he's small and fat, he dances amazingly **gracefully**.*

E *gracious:* 1. gütig, gnädig (oft ironisch); kultiviert (in der feststehenden Redewendung *gracious living*)

2. (Ausruf) Gracious! / Good gracious (me)! / Goodness gracious (me)! = Ach du meine Güte! / du grüne Neune (den engl. Ausrufen haftet heute etwas Altmodisch-Damenhaftes an.)

1. How **gracious** of her to visit our humble abode!	*Wie **gütig** von ihr, unsere bescheidene Hütte zu besuchen!*
2. **Gracious me**, the cat's asleep in the washbasin.	***Ach du meine Güte**, die Katze schläft im Waschbecken!*

GRINSEN / GRIN

G *grinsen* / E *grin:* sind oft äquivalent, aber es ist zu beachten, daß das engl. Wort im Gegensatz zum deutschen eher positiv als abwertend ist: vgl. folgende eindeutig abschätzigen engl. Verben.

grinsen (hämisch, höhnisch)	*to smirk*
grinsen (lüstern)	*to leer*

Das engl. *grin* wird oft besser durch *lächeln* oder *strahlen* übersetzt, wenn eine eindeutig freundliche Intention gemeint ist.

HACKEN / HACK

G *hacken:* 1. (Holz, Gemüse) to chop (up); (Fleisch) to mince
2. (sich schneiden) to cut (oneself)
3. (Blumenbeet usw.) to hoe
4. (bei Vögeln = picken) to peck
5. (mit einem spitzen Gerät schneiden, aushöhlen usw.) to hack
6. (Idiom) auf jmdm. herumhacken = *to keep going on at s.o., to keep getting at s.o., to pick on s.o.*

1. Mit diesem stumpfen Beil kannst du kein Holz **hacken**.

   *You can't **chop** wood with this blunt axe.*

   Ich weine immer, wenn ich Zwiebeln (klein) **hacke**.

   *I always cry when I **chop (up)** onions.*

   Auch **gehackt** war das Fleisch ungenießbar.

   *The meat was inedible even after it had been **minced**.*

   Hackfleisch

   mince**, **mincemeat, **minced** meat*

* Vorsicht! **Mincemeat** hat auch eine zweite kulinarische Bedeutung: eine süße Pastetenfüllung, bes. für 'mince pies' an Weihnachten.

2. Er **hackte** sich mit der Sichel ins linke Knie.

   *He **cut** his left knee with the sickle.*

3. Das ganze Unkraut hast du nur, weil du nie **hackst**.

   *The only reason you've got all these weeds is because you never **hoe**.*

4. Wenn du den Finger durch das Gitter steckst, wird der Kakadu hinein**hacken**.

   *If you put your finger through the bars, the cockatoo will **peck** it.*

   Hackordnung

   ***pecking** order*

5. Es gelang ihm, mit einem Spaten ein Loch in den harten Boden zu **hacken**.

   *He managed to **hack** a hole in the hard ground with a spade.*

   Er **hackte** zwei Äste ab.

   *He **hacked / cut** off two branches.*

6. Warum **hackt** der Chef immer auf mir **herum**?

   *Why does the boss keep **picking on** me / **getting at** me?*

E *hack:* siehe G5.

N.B.   a **hacking** cough

   *ein **trockener** (Reiz)husten*

HAUSEN, HAUSIEREN / HOUSE

G *hausen:*   1. (wohnen) to live, dwell (es gibt kein engl. Äquivalent, das eindeutig abwertend ist)
             2. (große Schäden anrichten) to wreak havoc, destruction

2. Überlebende erzählten davon, wie schrecklich die Rebellen in dieser Provinz **gehaust** hatten.	*Survivors related what **havoc** the rebels had **wrought** in this province.*

G *hausieren:* to peddle, hawk

Wie lange will er noch mit diesem pseudomarxistischen Blödsinn **hausieren**?	*How much longer is he going to keep **peddling** that pseudo-Marxist tripe?*
Hausieren verboten	*No **hawkers***

E *house:* to house s.o. = jmdn. unterbringen, jmdm. eine Wohnung / ein Heim / eine Unterkunft geben. Das engl. Verb ist immer transitiv.

Who's supposed to **house** all these refugees?	*Wer soll all diesen Flüchtlingen eine **Unterkunft** geben?*

HAUSHALT / HOUSEHOLD

G *Haushalt:*   1. (familienbezogen) household; (in bestimmten Kombinationen auch:) house, housework, housekeeping
              2. (Etat, Budget) budget
              3. (biol.) balance

1. Wie viele **Haushalte** gibt es in einem solchen Wohnblock?	*How many **households** are there in a block of flats like this?*
Sie muß arbeiten und den **Haushalt** führen.	*She has to work and run the **house(hold)** / do the **housework** / do the **housekeeping**.*
Seine Tante führt ihm den **Haushalt**.	*His aunt keeps **house** for him.*
Die Untersuchung zeigt, daß nur wenige Männer im **Haushalt** helfen.	*The study shows that only a few men help with the **housework**.*

2. Solche Ausgaben sind in unserem **Haushalt** nicht vorgesehen. *Our **budget** does not allow for such expenditure.*

3. den Hormon**haushalt** stören *to disturb the hormone **balance***

E *household:* siehe G1.

HAUSMANN / HOUSEMAN

G *Hausmann:* (male) "housewife", (noch sehr selten) househusband

Da ich letzten Monat meine Stelle verloren habe, meine Frau aber immer noch gut verdient, bin ich jetzt der **Hausmann**. *Since I lost my job last month but my wife still has a good income, I'm the "housewife" now.*

N.B. Der in vielen zweisprachigen Wörterbüchern angegebene - und durchaus logische - Ausdruck *househusband* ist bisher nicht in den alltäglichen Sprachgebrauch übernommen worden (vielleicht wegen männlichen Widerstandes?) und erscheint so gut wie nie in einsprachig Englischen Wörterbüchern.

E *houseman* /ˈhaʊsmən/: Assistenzarzt

N.B. Weil der Ausdruck *houseman* als gegen Frauen diskriminierend aufgefaßt werden kann, wird heute meist die neutrale Bezeichnung *house officer* vorgezogen.

HAUSMEISTER(IN) / HOUSEMASTER

G *Hausmeister(in):* caretaker

E *housemaster:* kein genaues Übersetzungsäquivalent. In engl. Internaten (bes. in den nichtstaatlichen *public schools*) werden die Schüler(innen) oft zwecks der Veranstaltung schulinterner Wettbewerbe (bes. sportlicher Art) verschiedenen 'houses' zugeteilt, die alle einen eigenen Namen tragen. *Housemaster(-mistress)* bezeichnet eine(n) einem bestimmten 'house' zugeteilte(n) Lehrer(in), der (die) bestimmte Pflichten in bezug auf Disziplin, Sicherheit usw. im 'house' wahrnimmt. Dieses System wurde auf ganz normale staatliche Tagesschulen übertragen.

HEFTIG / HEFTY

G *heftig:* fast nie durch *hefty* zu übersetzen. Die Wahl des entsprechenden Adjektivs hängt vom Zusammenhang ab - siehe Beispiele:

1. heftig = stark

heftige Kopfschmerzen	*severe / violent* headache
heftige(r) Regen(schauer)	*heavy rain / showers;* **driving** *rain*
heftiger Kampf	*fierce / violent struggle*
heftige Liebe	*violent / passionate love*
heftige Schmerzen	*intense / severe pain*

2. heftig = jähzornig

heftiger Mensch	*quick-tempered / (stärker)* **violent-tempered** *person*
heftig werden	*to lose one's temper / (stärker)* **to fly into a rage**

E *hefty:* meist informell im Stil.
1. (Mensch) kräftig; schwer
2. (Gegenstand) schwer
3. (Rechnung usw.) saftig

1. If I were you, I wouldn't pick a quarrel with a bloke as **hefty** as Big Joe.

   *Ich würde mich an deiner Stelle mit einem so **kräftigen** Typ wie Big Joe nicht anlegen.*

   Grandmother's pretty **hefty** - it's not easy to carry her.

   *Großmutter ist ganz schön **schwer** - es ist nicht leicht, sie zu tragen.*

2. The wardrobe was pretty **hefty**.

   *Der Kleiderschrank war ganz schön **schwer**.*

3. This tennis club charges a **hefty** joining fee.

   *Dieser Tennisklub verlangt eine **saftige** Aufnahmegebühr.*

HEILEN / HEAL

G *heilen:* 1.(Krankheit, Person) to cure
2.(Wunde) to heal

1. Wir können diese Krankheit zwar nicht **heilen**, aber wir können etwas gegen die Schmerzen tun.

   *Although we cannot **cure** this disease, we can do something about the pain.*

Von seinem Verfolgungswahn kann ihn kein Arzt **heilen**.	*No doctor can **cure** him of his persecution mania.*
2. Solche Wunden **heilen** nur langsam.	*Wounds like that take a long time to **heal**.*

E *heal:* siehe G2.

HINDERN / HINDER

G *hindern:*   1. (jmdn. von etwas abhalten) to prevent / stop (s.o. from doing s.th.)
               2. (behindern: Prozeß usw.) to hinder, hamper, impede
               3. (jmdn. bei einer Arbeit usw. stören) to hinder, be a hindrance

1. Keiner **hindert** Sie daran, zur Polizei zu gehen.	*No one's **stopping** you from going to the police.*
2. Solche Praktiken **hindern** schon lange das Wirtschaftswachstum.	*Such practices have been **hindering** / **hampering** economic growth for a long time.*
3. Er meint es zwar gut, aber er **hindert** mich an der Arbeit.	*I know he means well, but he does **hinder** me in my work.*

E *hinder:* siehe G2 und G3.

HONORIEREN / HONOUR

G *honorieren:*   1. (Honorar entrichten) to pay a fee (to s.o. for s.th.), remunerate (s.o. for s.th.)
                   2. (anerkennen) to honour, recognise, acknowledge

1. Er wurde für seine Arbeit in Saudi Arabien mit 20 000 Mark **honoriert**.	*He was **paid a fee** of 20,000 marks for his work in Saudi Arabia.*
Für diese äußerst wichtige Arbeit wurden sie bis jetzt meist sehr schlecht **honoriert**.	*Up to now they have been generally very poorly **remunerated** for this extremely important work.*

2. Zu seinen Lebzeiten wurde sein Beitrag nicht gebührend **honoriert**.

His contribution was not properly recognised / given proper recognition during his lifetime.

E *honour:* 1. (Mensch) **ehren; auszeichnen**
2. (Scheck, Wechsel, finanzielle oder vertragliche Verpflichtungen usw.) **annehmen, einhalten, honorieren**.

1. I was deeply **honoured** by your invitation to dinner.

Ich fühlte mich durch Ihre Einladung zum Diner zutiefst geehrt.

For this he was **honoured** with the Military Cross.

Dafür wurde er mit dem Military Cross ausgezeichnet.

2. If you don't **honour** your contract, we'll sue you.

Wenn Sie Ihren Vertrag nicht einhalten, werden wir Sie verklagen.

HUMAN / HUMAN

G *human:* 1. (menschenwürdig) **humane** /hjuːˈmeɪn/, **civilized**
2. (rücksichtsvoll, nachsichtig) **considerate, decent, understanding**
3. (med.) **human** /ˈhjuːmən/

1. Die Verhältnisse in solchen Gefängnissen sind relativ **human**.

The conditions in such prisons are relatively humane / civilized.

2. Bei diesem **humanen** Lehrer lernte ich viel schneller.

I learnt a lot quicker with this considerate / understanding teacher.

3. **Human**medizin

human medicine

E *human* /ˈhjuːmən/: **menschlich, ein Mensch**

He saved his own skin and abandoned the others: sad, but only **human**, I suppose.

Er hat seine eigene Haut gerettet und die anderen im Stich gelassen: traurig, aber wohl menschlich.

O.K., I forgot - I'm only **human**.

Na gut, ich hab's vergessen - ich bin ja auch nur ein Mensch.

INDIKATION / INDICATION

G *Indikation:* 1. (med., in bezug auf Gründe für Schwangerschaftsabbruch) Umschreibung mit *on* .... *grounds*
2. (med., bei Therapien, Arzneimitteln usw.) indication (Das engl. Wort gehört in diesem Sinne eindeutig der Fachsprache an.)

1. Eine **medizinische Indikation** für einen Schwangerschaftsabbruch akzeptiere ich, nicht aber eine **soziale**.

*I accept abortion / termination of pregnancy **on medical**, but not **on social grounds**.*

E *indication:* 1. (An)zeichen, Hinweis
2. siehe G2.

1. Is there any **indication** that he will change his mind?

*Gibt es irgendeinen **Hinweis** dafür, daß er seine Meinung ändern wird?*

For days now there have been unmistakeable **indications** of a world economic crisis.

*Seit Tagen gibt es unübersehbare **Anzeichen** für eine Weltwirtschaftskrise.*

INSERIEREN / INSERT

G *inserieren:* to advertise (Inserat = advertisement, (ugs.) advert, ad)

Wenn du in der Zeitung **inserierst**, wirst du das Auto vielleicht los.

*If you **advertise / put an ad(vert)** in the paper, you may get rid of your car.*

Ich habe wegen des Kühlschranks viermal in der Zeitung **inseriert**, aber keiner hat sich gemeldet.

*I've **advertised** the fridge in the paper four times, but no one's been in touch.*

E *insert:* hineinstecken, einwerfen, einführen, einschieben

If you **insert** the wrong coin, of course the machine won't work.

*Wenn du die falsche Münze **einwirfst**, wird der Automat natürlich nicht funktionieren.*

Perhaps we ought to **insert** another paragraph.

*Vielleicht sollten wir noch einen Absatz **einschieben**.*

INSPEKTION / INSPECTION

G *Inspektion:* 1. (Kfz.) service; Umschreibung mit *to be serviced*
2. (Überprüfung allgemein) inspection

1. Ich bin nächste Woche nicht da - kannst du das Auto zur **Inspektion** bringen?
   *I'm not here next week - can you take the car in for a **service** / **to be serviced**?*

2. Eine **Inspektion** der Fabrik ergab verschiede gravierende Verstöße gegen die gesetzlichen Vorschriften.
   *An **inspection** of the factory revealed various serious infringements of the legal regulations.*

E *inspection:* Kontrolle, Überprüfung, Untersuchung, Inspektion: vgl. G2. Das engl. Wort wird viel häufiger als das deutsche verwendet.

INSTANZ / INSTANCE

G *Instanz:* 1. (jur.) "instance", aber diese Bedeutung des Wortes ist den meisten Laien unbekannt: in nichtfachsprachlichen Texten sind andere Ausdrücke vorzuziehen (siehe Beispiele)
2. (Behörde usw.) authority, department

1. Sie gewann den Prozeß **in der zweiten Instanz**.
   *She won the case **at the second hearing** / **on appeal**.*

   Er ist bereit, den Prozeß **durch alle Instanzen** hindurch zu führen.
   *He's prepared to fight the case **through the courts** / (in GB) to take the case **as far as the House of Lords**.*

2. Keiner konnte mir sagen, an welche **Instanz** ich mich wenden sollte.
   *No one could tell me what **authority** / **department** to apply to.*

E *instance:* 1. Beispiel
2. in the first instance = zunächst; erstens
   in the second instance = zweitens

1. This is a good **instance** of the sort of delay bureaucracy can cause.
   *Dies ist ein gutes **Beispiel** für die Art von Verzögerung, die die Bürokratie verursachen kann.*

INTELLIGENZ / INTELLIGENCE

G *Intelligenz:* 1. (Denkfähigkeit) intelligence
2. (Gesamtheit der Intellektuellen) intelligentsia
/ɪnˌtelɪˈdʒentsɪə/

1. Was hilft uns seine **Intelligenz**, wenn er faul ist?
 *What good is his **intelligence** to us if he's lazy?*

2. Es fehlte der **Intelligenz** an politischem Engagement.
 *The **intelligentsia** lacked political commitment.*

E *intelligence:* 1. siehe G1.
2. (über den Geheimdienst usw. erworbene) Informationen
3. Nachrichtendienst, Geheimdienst

2. According to our latest **intelligence**, enemy units have landed on the island.
 *Unseren letzten **Informationen** zufolge sind feindliche Verbände auf der Insel gelandet.*

3. He worked for British **intelligence** during the war.
 *Im Krieg arbeitete er für den britischen **Nachrichtendienst** / **Geheimdienst**.*

JUBILÄUM / JUBILEE

G *Jubiläum:* (x-jähriges Bestehen; Dienst-) anniversary (oder Umschreibung); jubilee /ˈdʒuːbɪˈliː/ (siehe E *jubilee*)

Der Schützenverein feierte im vergangenen Jahr sein zehnjähriges **Jubiläum**.
*The shooting club celebrated its tenth **anniversary** last year.*

Nächstes Jahr feiere ich mein **30jähriges Jubiläum** in der Firma.
*Next year I'll be celebrating **30 years with the firm**.*

E *jubilee:* Das Wort wird heute nicht mehr sehr oft benutzt, außer in den feststehenden Kombinationen *silver jubilee* (25jähriges Jubiläum), *golden jubilee* (50jähriges Jubiläum) und *diamond jubilee* (60jähriges Jubiläum) in bezug auf die Länge der Herrschaft eines Monarchen/einer Monarchin.

SECTION D - EXERCISES

A. Translate the words in brackets so that they fit into the sentences.

1. Some hours after leaving the Persian .... (Golf), we flew over the .... (Golf) of Biscay.

2. Filbert has always been an extremely .... (graziös) dancer.

3. He always uses .... (human) ways of putting sick animals to sleep.

4. Do you think you could take the car in ....(zur Inspektion)?

5. Of course we'll have to .... (honorieren) such a highly qualified lecturer - he won't do it for nothing.

6. Why does he keep .... (hausieren) this nonsense about inner happiness?

7. Tomorrow is the thirtieth .... (Jubiläum) of the founding of The Pinky Winky Club.

8. Poor Tom is full of good intentions, but whenever he comes here, he only manages to .... (hindern) me in my work.

9. A .... (grandios) dinner-dance has been arranged in honour of our returning Olympic athletes.

10. I didn't notice anything, but apparently the .... (Hausmeister) saw someone lurking suspiciously near the school gates.

B. TRUE OR FALSE? Mark the following sentences T or F in the space provided. Write corrections for the false statements on the right.

	T	F	CORRECTION
1. If someone grins at you, it can't show a positive feeling.			
2. 'Intelligence' and 'intelligentsia' are synonyms.			
3. To sell something, you can insert it in a newspaper.			
4. Councils which are short of money are on a tight budget.			
5. Farmers hack round their vegetables to remove the weeds.			
6. Deep wounds can take a long time to heal.			
7. In some restaurants you can run up a hefty bill.			

C. Match the words on the left with their meanings on the right.

(a) indication   (1) to hawk
(b) jubilee   (2) a problem
(c) grandiose   (3) embarrassing
(d) to house   (4) a reason for terminating a pregnancy
(e) graceful   (5) tremendous or wonderful
(f) fatal   (6) quick-tempered or violent
(g) grand   (7) heavy
(h) crux   (8) to accommodate
(i) to peddle   (9) death-bringing
(j) hefty   (10) a sign
                      (11) pretentious, ostentatious or overdone
                      (12) anniversary of monarch's reign or lengthy marriage
                      (13) anniversary (general)
                      (14) to live or dwell
                      (15) gracious or highly cultivated
                      (16) essential point; the heart of the matter
                      (17) elegant

D. Translate the following phrases and sentences:

1. eine nette Clique
2. im Akkord arbeiten
3. An welche Instanz kann ich mich wenden?
4. Sie stellen nur Akademiker ein.
5. das Existenzminimum
6. Sie hat Staralllüren.
7. Das wissen wir noch nicht definitiv.
8. Diese Stadt hat ein bestimmtes Flair.

E. YES OR NO? Answer the following "Yes" or "No" - if "No", say why not.

	YES	NO	IF 'NO', WHY NOT?
1. Can a company frank a letter?			
2. Do camcorders have different formats?			
3. Can it become a chore to sing in a choir?			
4. Do decorators normally dress windows?			
5. Are exhibitionists usually arrested if seen by the police?			
6. Is it possible to make a frivolous remark?			
7. Could a brutal person act inhumanly?			
8. Do people write differentiated reports?			

SECTION E

JUSTIZ / JUSTICE

G *Justiz:* (die Gerichte) the courts;
(das Gerichtswesen) the judiciary /djuː'dɪʃəri/

In solchen Fällen ist die **Justiz** machtlos.   *The courts are / The judiciary is powerless in such cases.*

E *justice:* 1. Gerechtigkeit
2. Richter (bei bestimmten Amtsbezeichnungen)

1. There's no **justice** in this country any more.   *In diesem Land gibt es keine Gerechtigkeit mehr.*

2. **justice** of the peace (J.P.)   *Friedensrichter (ehrenamtlicher Laienrichter)*
   Mr. **Justice** Simmonds   *Richter Simmonds*
   (The) Lord Chief **Justice**   *der oberste Richter (G.B.)*

KANONE / CANNON, CANON

G *Kanone:* 1. (Geschütz) gun; (älteres Geschütz, mit Kugeln usw. als Geschossen) cannon (pl.: cannon)
2. (ugs.: Revolver) gun, (coll.) shooter
3. (ugs., bes. Sport: Könner) ace, great / top player
4. unter aller Kanone = really awful, (meist AmE) the pits

1. Unsere neueste **Kanone** hat eine Reichweite von über 60 Kilometern.   *Our latest gun has got a range of over 60 kilometres.*

   Im alten Schloß gibt es mehrere **Kanonen** aus dem siebzehnten Jahrhundert.   *There are several seventeenth-century cannon in the old castle.*

2. Bist du wahnsinnig? Wieso nimmst du eine **Kanone** mit?   *Are you crazy? Why are you taking a gun / shooter?*

3. Er hat zwar nie ein Examen bestanden, ist aber als Tennisspieler eine **Kanone**.   *Although he's never passed an exam, he's a great tennis player / a tennis ace.*

4. Das Essen hier ist **unter aller Kanone**.   *The food here is really terrible / really awful / the pits.*

E *cannon:* siehe G1; bezeichnet auch bestimmte (moderne) automatische Bordwaffen größeren Kalibers, bes. bei Flugzeugen.

E *canon:* 1. Kanoniker / Kanonikus
2. Kanon

KAPAZITÄT / CAPACITY

G *Kapazität:* 1. (jmd. mit hervorragenden Fachkenntnissen) (recognized) expert / authority, leading figure
2. (sonst) capacity /kəˈpæsəti/

1. Kaum zu glauben, daß dieser unscheinbare kleine Mann eine **Kapazität** auf dem Gebiet der Kernfusion war.

It was difficult to believe that this inconspicuous little man was an **authority** *in the field of nuclear fusion.*

E *capacity:* 1. Kapazität (aber nicht im Sinne von G1); (Motor) Hubraum; Fassungsvermögen (eines Behälters); *capacity crowd* und *capacity audience* drücken den Begriff 'ausverkauft' aus
2. (bei Arbeitsbeschreibung usw.) Funktion, Eigenschaft
3. Fähigkeit

1. We always play to **capacity** crowds.

Bei uns ist jedes Spiel **ausverkauft**.

2. In my **capacity** as your lawyer I must advise you against it.

(In meiner **Eigenschaft**) *als Ihr Anwalt muß ich Ihnen davon abraten.*

3. His **capacity** for surviving against all expectations is amazing.

Seine **Fähigkeit**, *entgegen allen Erwartungen zu überleben, ist erstaunlich.*

KARIKATUR / CARICATURE

G *Karikatur:* 1. (individuelle Zeichnung) cartoon /kaːˈtuːn/
2. (sonst meist) caricature /ˈkærɪkəˌtʃʊə/

1. Auf Seite 10 fand der Minister eine nicht sehr schmeichelhafte **Karikatur**, die ihn mit einer großen Nase darstellte.

On page 10 the Minister found a not very flattering **cartoon** *that depicted him with a big nose.*

2. Diese Zusammenfassung ist eine **Karikatur** dessen, was ich gesagt habe.

This summary is a **caricature** *of what I said.*

E *caricature:* siehe *nur* G2.

KARNEVAL / CARNIVAL

G *Karneval* / E *carnival* /ˈkɑːnɪvəl/: Obwohl dt. *Karneval* traditionell mit engl. *carnival* übersetzt wird, bezeichnet das engl. Wort in einem englischen Kontext eine ganz andere Art Feier. Ein *carnival* wird meist für wohltätige Zwecke veranstaltet; Hauptattraktion dabei ist der Festzug. Feuchtfröhliche Ausgelassenheit über einen längeren Zeitraum hat mit einem englischen *carnival* nichts zu tun. Dieser gleicht eher einem Volksfest - ohne Alkohol - und nimmt in der Regel nur einen Nachmittag in Anspruch.

KERN / KERNEL

G *Kern:* 1. (eines Atoms) nucleus /ˈnjuːklɪəs/; Kern- = nuclear / atomic
2. (Problem usw.) heart, core, crux; (selten) kernel
3. (Obst, Nüsse):

      pip   (klein - bei Äpfeln, Orangen usw.)
      seed   (klein und in großen Mengen vorhanden:
               bei Kürbissen, Melonen usw.)
      stone   (groß, einzeln: bei Pflaumen, Pfirsichen,
               Kirschen, Aprikosen usw.)
      kernel (bei Nüssen)

4. Stadtkern = town centre, city centre

1. **Kern**waffen   *nuclear / atomic* weapons
   Kernkraftwerk   ***nuclear*** power station

2. Ja, das ist der **Kern** der Sache: dieses   Yes, that's the ***heart*** of the matter: this
   Gefälle zwischen arm und reich.   gap between rich and poor.

E *kernel* /ˈkɜːnəl/: Kern (von einer Nuß, von einem Stein usw.); siehe auch G2.

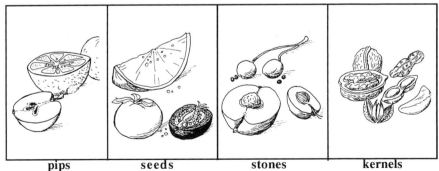

pips	seeds	stones	kernels
(oranges, apples, lemons, grapes, etc.)	(melons, tomatoes, pumpkins, etc.)	(peaches, apricots, cherries, plums, etc.)	(mainly nuts)

KITT / KIT

G *Kitt:* (Fensterkitt) putty /'pʌti/

E *kit:* 1.(bei verschiedenen Geräten, die zusammengehören):
tool kit = Werkzeug(satz)
repair kit = Reparatursatz
first aid kit = Verbandskasten, Erste-Hilfe-Ausrüstung
football kit = Fußballsachen usw.
2. Bastelsatz, Bausatz (für Modellflugzeuge usw.)
3. Ausrüstung (eines Soldaten)

KLAPPEN / CLAP

G *klappen:* 1.(zusammen-) to fold (up, away, etc.)
2.(scharnierartig bewegen) to lift up, raise
3.(ugs., gelingen) to succeed (formell); (ugs.) to work out, come off, go all right, go O.K. (sowie verschiedene andere stark kontextgebundene Fügungen)

1. Kannst du bitte den Stuhl für mich **zusammenklappen**?

   *Can you **fold up** the chair for me, please?*

2. Bei solchen Katzentüren wird dieses Teil ganz einfach vom Kopf der Katze **nach oben geklappt**, wenn sie hereinkommt oder hinausgeht.

   *With cat-flaps of this type this part is quite simply **lifted up** by the cat's head when the cat comes in or goes out.*

3. Hat es mit deinem Examen **geklappt**?

   *Did your exam **go O.K.**?*

   Zwischen Beate und ihm **hat** es **nie** so richtig **geklappt**.

   *Things **never went well** between Beate and him.*

E *clap:* (Beifall) klatschen

They all **clapped** when he stood up.   *Sie **klatschten** alle, als er aufstand.*

KOMMA / COMMA

G *Komma:* 1. (meist) comma
2. (bei Dezimalzahlen) point (Im Engl. wird Punkt statt Komma verwendet.)

2. 8,73 - in Worten: acht **Komma** sieben drei. *8.73 - in words: eight **point** seven three.*

E *comma:* siehe *nur* G1.

KOMMANDIEREN / COMMAND, COMMANDEER

G *kommandieren:* 1. (herum-) to order around / about, to boss around / about
2. (das Kommando haben) to command, be in command of, (im Passiv auch: to be commanded by)
3. (ab-) to post, to second /sɪˈkɒnd/

1. Das ist aber schlimm, wie deine Großmutter die ganze Familie **herumkommandiert**. *It's awful the way your grandmother **bosses** the whole family **around**.*

2. Keiner scheint zu wissen, wer diese Truppe **kommandiert**. *No one seems to know who **is in command of** this troop.*

3. Ich möchte nicht an die Hauptstelle **abkommandiert** werden - ich kenne dort niemanden. *I wouldn't like to be **posted** to Head Office - I don't know anyone there.*

E *to command* /kəˈmɑːnd/: 1. befehlen
2. to command a (good) view of s.th. = eine schöne Aussicht auf etwas bieten

E *to commandeer* /ˌkɒmənˈdɪə/: **requirieren**

All lorries were **commandeered** by the army. *Alle Lkws wurden vom Heer requiriert.*

KOMMANDO / COMMANDO

G *Kommando:* 1. (military / military-style) order, command
2. authority, Umschreibung mit *in command*
3. (military) unit; (weniger oft) commando

1. Er gab uns das **Kommando** zum Schießen.

   *He gave us the **order / command** to shoot.*

2. Fletcher hat hier das **Kommando**.

   *Fletcher is **in command** here.*

3. Das Spezial**kommando** bekam den Auftrag, die Innenstadt zu räumen.

   *The special **unit** was given the task of clearing the town centre.*

E *commando* /kə'mɑːndəʊ/: Angehöriger / Mitglied eines Kommandotrupps

The **commandos** scaled the wall and attacked the village.

*Die **Angehörigen des Kommandotrupps** erkletterten die Mauer und griffen das Dorf an.*

KOMMISSION / COMMISSION

G *Kommission:* Allgemein ist festzustellen, daß *commission* als Übersetzung nur zutreffend ist, wenn größere Untersuchungskommissionen (meist auf nationaler Ebene) gemeint sind. Bei kleineren, z.B. hochschulinternen Gremien ist *committee* passender; manchmal sind andere Ausdrücke gebräuchlicher.

Die **Kommission** wird das Problem der Schwarzarbeit in Deutschland untersuchen.

*The **Commission** will investigate the problem of moonlighting in Germany.*

die EG-**Kommission**

*the EC **Commission***

Ich bin Mitglied in so vielen **Kommissionen**, daß ich für die Forschung keine Zeit mehr habe.

*I'm a member of so many **committees** that I no longer have any time for research.*

Prüfungskommission

examination board / board of examiners

E *commission* /kə'mɪʃən/: 1. Provision
2. Auftrag (für Architekten usw.)
3. Begehen (eines Verbrechens)
4. Offizierspatent

1. I won't earn much on 2% **commission**!   *Bei einer **Provision** von 2% werde ich nicht viel verdienen!*

2. He couldn't believe it - he had been given the **commission** for the new court-house.   *Er konnte es nicht glauben - man hatte ihm den **Auftrag** für das neue Gerichtsgebäude gegeben.*

KOMMUNE / COMMUNE

G *Kommune:*   1. (Verwaltung: Gemeinde) local authority, (Stadt auch) municipal /mjuːˈnɪsɪpəl/ authority
                2. (von Personen mit alternativem Lebensstil usw.) commune
                3. die Pariser Kommune = the Paris Commune

1. Solche Entscheidungen werden zu 60 Prozent von den **Kommunen** und nicht vom Bund oder von den Bundesländern getroffen.   *60 per cent of such decisions are taken by the **local authorities**, and not by the federal government or the federal states.*

E *commune* /ˈkɒmjuːn/: siehe G2 und G3.

KOMPETENT / COMPETENT

G *kompetent:*   1. (zuständig) responsible
                2. (fähig, sachverständig) competent /ˈkɒmpɪtənt/

1. Keiner konnte mir sagen, welche Behörde für solche Fragen **kompetent** ist.   *No one could tell me which authority is **responsible** for such matters.*

E *competent:* fähig. Das engl. Wort hat zwar auch die Bedeutung *zuständig*, aber die Bedeutung *fähig* ist weitaus häufiger. *Competent* im Sinne von *zuständig* kann also leicht mißverstanden werden.

I have dismissed the doctor: he's quite simply not **competent**.   *Den Arzt habe ich entlassen: er ist ganz einfach **unfähig**.*

NB. Die Negativform *incompetent* hat in der modernen Umgangssprache nur den Sinn *unfähig*.

KONDENSMILCH / CONDENSED MILK

G *Kondensmilch* / E *condensed milk:* Die englische *condensed milk* ist in Deutschland fast unbekannt: sie ist zähflüssiger und stärker gesüßt als die deutsche Kondensmilch.

| Kondensmilch | *evaporated milk* /ɪˈvæpəˌreɪtɪd/ |
| condensed milk | *sehr dicke, zähflüssige Kondensmilch* |

KONFEKTION / CONFECTION

G *Konfektion:* (production of) ready-to-wear, ready-made clothing / clothes; off-the-peg clothing / clothes

Ich kann keine **Konfektionsware** kaufen: Nichts scheint mir zu passen.	*I can't buy **ready-made clothes**: nothing seems to fit me.*
In der **Konfektionsbranche** sind jetzt viele Prozesse computergesteuert.	*Many processes are now computer-controlled in the production of **ready-to-wear clothing**.*
Konfektionsgröße	*size*

E *confectionery* /kənˈfekʃnri/: Süßigkeiten, Süßwaren; (hohe Qualität) Konfekt

| **Confectionery** is bad for your teeth. | ***Süßigkeiten** sind schlecht für die Zähne.* |

KONSERVE / CONSERVE

G *Konserve:* 1. (Lebensmittel in Dosen) tinned food, (AmE) canned food
2. (Dose) tin, (AmE; BrE bes. für Getränke) can
3. (übertr.) aus der Konserve = canned

1. Wenn du nur von **Konserven** lebst, Tommy, fehlen dir die Vitamine.
   *If you only eat **tinned food / canned food**, Tommy, you won't get enough vitamins.*

2. Der Kofferraum war voller **Konserven**.
   *The boot (AmE: trunk) was full of **tins / cans**.*

3. Unterhaltung **aus der Konserve** *canned* entertainment
   Musik **aus der Konserve** *muzak, canned music*

E *conserve* /ˈkɒnsɜːv/: Konfitüre von bes. hoher Qualität, mit ganzen Früchten. Kommt eher in Markennamen als in der Umgangssprache vor.

KONSTRUKTEUR(IN) / CONSTRUCTOR
KONSTRUKTION / CONSTRUCTION

G *Konstrukteur(in):* designer, design engineer

G *Konstruktion:* 1. (Entwurf) design
2. (sonst meist) construction

E *constructor:* "Erbauer": das engl. Wort ist ungebräuchlich und wird am besten nicht benutzt.

E *construction:* Bau; Konstruktion (wenn nicht das Entwerfen gemeint ist)

KONZENTRIERT / CONCENTRATED

G *konzentriert:* 1. (geistige Konzentration zeigend) Umschreibung mit *to concentrate* oder *concentration*
2. (chem.; sonst) concentrated

1. Ich kann nicht **konzentriert** arbeiten - ich brauche Ruhe. *I can't **concentrate** on my work - I need some peace and quiet.*

   Der Junge arbeitet sehr **konzentriert** und lernt schnell. *The boy works with a great deal of **concentration** and is learning fast.*

2. Die Aufstellung von Raketen, auf ein kleines Gebiet **konzentriert**, hat zu großer Besorgnis geführt. *The deployment of missiles, **concentrated** on a small area, has led to grave concern.*

   konzentrierte Schwefelsäure ***concentrated** sulphuric acid*

E *concentrated:* siehe *nur* G2.

KONZEPT / CONCEPT

G *Konzept:*   1. (Entwurf) **draft**
                2. (Programm) **plan, programme** (AmE **program**), **scheme**; (Idiome) siehe Beispiele

1. Er hat sein **Konzept** schon dreimal überarbeitet.
     *He's already been over his **draft** three times.*

2. Wir brauchen ein völlig neues **Konzept**, um mit diesem Problem fertig zu werden.
     *We need an entirely new **scheme** / **plan** to deal with this problem.*

Nach dieser Unterbrechung **geriet er völlig aus dem Konzept**.
     *After this interruption **he** completely **lost his thread**.*

Jetzt hast du mich **aus dem Konzept gebracht**!
     *Now you've **put me off**!*

Das wird unserem Minister nicht **ins Konzept passen**.
     *That won't **fit in with** our Minister's **plans**.*

E *concept* /'kɒnsept/: **Begriff, Idee, Vorstellung**

A child of this age does not understand such abstract **concepts**.
     *Ein Kind in diesem Alter versteht solche abstrakten **Begriffe** nicht.*

KONZERT / CONCERT

G *Konzert:*   1. (musikal. Veranstaltung) **concert** /'kɒnsət/; (bei Solisten auch:) **recital** /rɪ'saɪtəl/
                2. (Klavier-, Violin- usw.) **concerto** /kən'tʃeətəʊ/

1. Bei solchen Pop**konzerten** gibt es keine numerierten Sitzplätze.
     *There aren't any numbered seats at pop **concerts** of this sort.*

Ich habe eine Karte für das Brendel-**Konzert** ergattert.
     *I've managed to get hold of a ticket for the Brendel **recital**.*

2. Ich habe eine CD mit Flöten**konzerten** von Vivaldi gekauft.
     *I've bought a CD of Vivaldi flute **concertos**.*

E *concert:*   1. siehe G1.
               2. (to act / work) **in concert with** s.o. = mit jmdm. zusammen (handeln / arbeiten)

SECTION E - EXERCISES

A. *Translate the words in brackets so that they fit into the sentences.*

1. Ann is now a(n)..................... (Kapazität) in the field of laser surgery.

2. Are you prepared to .... (attestieren) that this prisoner is unfit to plead in court?

3. The reason why she gets on everyone's nerves is that she constantly tries to .... (Leute herumkommandieren).

4. I wandered round the building for nearly an hour, but I didn't manage to find the person who was .... (kompetent) for dealing with such problems.

5. I'm afraid I've got to phone the garage; my car was .... (demoliert) during the night and I need to get it fixed as soon as possible.

6. The final .... (Konzept) of Peter's speech looks very impressive.

7. Have you heard the news? It's awful. Felicity was killed last night in a .... (Frontalzusammenstoß).

8. Yes - this report gets to the very .... (Kern) of the problem.

9. Do you seriously believe that the .... (Kommune) is going to put up the money for a new outdoor swimming-pool?

10. This is a ....(demonstrativ) example of his pig-headedness.

11. Eve wants to be a model, but I'm afraid she hasn't got the ....(Figur) for it.

12. Oswald is studying to be a(n) .... (Konstrukteur).

13. When the professor gets drunk at the departmental parties, he almost becomes a(n) .... (Karikatur) of himself.

14. He's been .... (exerzieren) those troops for three hours now.

15. She's happiest when Cedric takes her to some ....(feudal) restaurant.

16. This new wonder-drug is said to ....(heilen) 20 different diseases.

17. The burglars got in by removing the .... (Kitt) and taking the glass out.

18. There's not much that the .... (Justiz) can do in cases like that.

19. When I read who was on the .... (Prüfungskommission), I nearly had a heart attack.

20. John! .... (Zusammenklappen) that picnic chair and put it in the car!

B. Match the words on the left with their meanings on the right.

1. confectionery
2. canon
3. concerto
4. commission
5. cannon
6. kernel
7. concentrated
8. concept
9. commune
10. to commandeer

(a) to requisition
(b) the stone in certain fruits, e.g. cherry or apricot
(c) an idea or a notion
(d) full of concentration, paying attention
(e) to order s.o. around
(f) an expert or ace, e.g. at a certain sport
(g) a high-ranking officer in the army
(h) a concert
(i) an examination board
(j) a living unit, e.g. five people in one house
(k) a rough draft or plan, e.g. for a speech
(l) a kind of priest
(m) money earned as an agent for selling goods or services
(n) a musical composition for orchestra and 1 or 2 soloists
(o) ready-to-wear clothing
(p) the edible part of a nut, inside the shell
(q) one or more guns which can fire heavy metal balls
(r) sweets
(s) made more dense, intense or pure
(t) a local authority, e.g. a town council

C. Translate the following words, phrases and sentences:

1. sechs Komma sieben
2. null Komma vier
3. Man kauft Kondensmilch in Dosen.
4. Die Justiz kann Ihnen nicht helfen.
5. Das Essen war unter aller Kanone.
6. Wer ist für solche Angelegenheiten kompetent?
7. Kirschkerne sind größer als Weintraubenkerne.
8. Hackfleisch
9. Du hast einen Doppelgänger!
10. Lampenfieber
11. Seine Kleidung ist extravagant.
12. Er wurde exemplarisch bestraft.

SECTION F

KORN / KORN

G *Korn:* 1. piece, grain, speck: siehe Beispiele
2. (Getreide allgemein) grain, (seltener) corn
3. (Schnaps): kein engl. Äquivalent: *"corn schnapps"*

1. Staub**korn**   *speck / piece of dust*
    Hagel**korn**   *hailstone*
    Salz**korn** / Sand**korn**   *grain of salt / sand*

2. Wann wird das **Korn** geerntet?   *When will the grain be harvested?*

E *corn:* 1. (AmE) Mais (= BrE maize; der Ausdruck *corn on the cob* (= Maiskolben) wird aber auch im BrE benutzt); (BrE) vage Bezeichnung - von vielen für gleichbedeutend mit *wheat* (= Weizen) gehalten; vgl. G2.

2. Hühnerauge

KORRESPONDENT(IN) / CORRESPONDENT

G *Korrespondent(in):* 1. (für Fremdsprachenkorrespondent[in]) bilingual / multilingual secretary
2. (sonst) correspondent

E *correspondent:* siehe G2. Auch durchaus geläufig als Bezeichnung für jmdn., mit dem man einen Briefwechsel führt.

N.B. *Correspondent* /ˌkɒrɪˈspɒndənt/
      Co-respondent /ˌkəʊrɪˈspɒndənt/

Correspondent darf nicht mit *co-respondent* (Mitbeklagte(r) in einem Scheidungsprozeß) verwechselt werden! Siehe **ZITIEREN / CITE**, Seite 150, E1.

KOSTÜM / COSTUME

G *Kostüm:* 1. (zweiteiliges Kleidungsstück für Frauen) (two-piece) suit
2. (hist., theat.) costume; (Verkleidung auch) fancy dress

1. Warum trägt jede Frau in diesem Büro ein dunkles **Kostüm**?

   Why does every woman in this office wear a dark suit?

2. Diese römischen **Kostüme** wirken nicht sehr echt.

   These Roman costumes don't seem very authentic.

Kostümball
Kostümfilm

fancy-dress ball
period film / picture

E *costume* /ˈkɒstjuːm/: siehe G2.

swimming **costume**
bathing **costume** /ˈbeɪðɪŋ ˈkɒstjuːm/

Badeanzug
Badeanzug

KRIMINALITÄT / CRIMINALITY

G *Kriminalität:* crime (als Kollektivbegriff)

Die wachsende **Kriminalität** in den Innenstädten scheint ein unlösbares Problem zu sein.

The increasing crime in the inner cities appears to be an insoluble problem.

E *criminality:* (selten) bezeichnet die kriminelle Eigenschaft (einer Handlung usw.) - Umschreibung mit *kriminell*

There can be no doubt about the **criminality** of such an action.

Es besteht kein Zweifel daran, daß eine solche Handlung kriminell ist.

KUR / CURE

G *Kur:* 1. (Heilverfahren, allgemein) (course of) treatment
2. (an einem Kurort durchgeführt) health cure

1. Zu dieser **Kur** gegen Akne gehört viel Fruchtsaft.

   This (course of) treatment for acne includes lots of fruit juice.

2. Jedes Jahr fuhr er nach Bad Dürrheim zur **Kur**.

   Every year he went to Bad Dürrheim to take a health cure.

E *cure:* **Heilmittel**

There's no **cure** for this type of cancer.   *Gegen diese Art Krebs gibt es kein*
Heilmittel.

N.B. Die engl. Übersetzung für G2 ist nur eine Annäherung an das Phänomen der vom Arzt empfohlenen und von der Krankenkasse mitbezahlten Kur. Dies ist in Großbritannien fast unbekannt.

LAND / LAND

G *Land:* 1. (Staat: Frankreich, Italien usw.) country, (gehobener Stil) land
         2. (Bundesland) (federal) state
         3. (Land, nicht Wasser; Erdboden, für landwirtschaftliche Zwecke usw.; bei Großgrundbesitz) land
         4. (Land im Gegensatz zur Stadt) country, countryside

1. Sechs **Länder**, darunter auch Albanien, haben diesen Vertrag unterschrieben.   *Six **countries**, including Albania, have signed this treaty.*

   das Gelobte **Land**   *the Promised **Land***

2. Wie viele (Bundes)**länder** hat Österreich?   *How many (federal) **states** does Austria consist of?*

3. Wegen der starken Strömung konnte er nicht an **Land** schwimmen und ertrank.   *He was unable to reach **land** because of the strong current, and he drowned.*

   Welcher Bauer möchte solch sumpfiges **Land** kaufen?   *What farmer would want to buy this sort of marshy **land**?*

   Er besitzt noch viel **Land** in Italien.   *He still owns a lot of **land** in Italy.*

4. Warum sollte ich auf dem **Land** wohnen, wo ich doch so gern ins Kino und in die Kneipe gehe?   *Why should I live in the **country** when I enjoy going to the cinema and the pub so much?*

E *land:* siehe nur G1 und G3.

LANDSCHAFT / LANDSCAPE

G *Landschaft:* 1. (allgemein) countryside, (malerisch auch) scenery;
(breiter Landstrich, von einem Punkt aus gesehen) landscape
2. (Gemälde) landscape

1. Die **Landschaft** in dieser Gegend ist zwar ganz schön, aber nichts Besonderes.

    *The **countryside** round here is quite nice, but nothing special.*

    Ich fahre wegen der **Landschaft** in die Schweiz.

    *I go to Switzerland for the **scenery**.*

    Wir erreichten die Spitze des Turmes: eine öde, windgepeitschte **Landschaft** lag uns zu Füßen.

    *We reached the top of the tower: a bleak, windswept **landscape** lay at our feet.*

2. Der Wert dieser **Landschaften** von Van Gogh ist erheblich gestiegen.

    *The value of these **landscapes** by Van Gogh has increased considerably.*

E *landscape:* siehe G1 und G2.

LAUT / LOUD

G *laut:* 1. (Person, Ort) noisy
2. (Musik, Stimme, Fernsehen u.ä.) loud

1. Die Kinder sind eigentlich ganz nett, aber sehr **laut**.

    *They're actually quite nice children, but they're very **noisy**.*

    Wir wohnen an einer großen Kreuzung im Zentrum, und es ist daher sehr **laut**.

    *We live at a big junction in the centre, and because of that it's very **noisy**.*

2. Die Musik in der Disko war viel zu **laut**.

    *The music in the disco was far too **loud**.*

E *loud:* 1. Siehe G2.
2. (abwertend, in bezug auf Farben und Muster sowie menschliches Verhalten) grell, aufdringlich

2. He was wearing a very **loud** red tie.

    *Er trug einen **grell**roten Schlips.*

    His inferiority complex expresses itself in **loud** behaviour.

    *Sein Minderwertigkeitskomplex äußert sich in **aufdringlichem** Verhalten.*

LEXIKON / LEXICON

G *Lexikon:* 1. (Enzyklopädie) encyclopaedia; (Nachschlagewerk zu einem bestimmten Wissensgebiet: auch) dictionary
2. (Wörterbuch) dictionary; (für alte Sprachen: auch) lexicon
3. (Linguistik) lexicon

1. In dieser Wohnung haben wir für ein 25-bändiges **Lexikon** keinen Platz.

   *We haven't got any room for a 25-volume **encyclopaedia** in this flat.*

   Sein **Lexikon** der Psychologie ist auch als Taschenbuch erhältlich.

   *His **Dictionary** of Psychology is also available in paperback.*

2. Mein Großvater hat mir dieses Deutsch-Italienisch-**Lexikon** geschenkt.

   *My grandfather gave me this German-Italian **dictionary**.*

   Ohne Zweifel ist dies das beste Deutsch-Latein-**Lexikon**.

   *Without a doubt this is the best German-Latin **dictionary** / **lexicon**.*

E *lexicon:* siehe G2 und G3.

LOKAL / LOCAL

G *Lokal (n.):* pub, bar, restaurant (je nach Angebot und Ausstattung)

G *lokal (adj.):* local

E *local (n.)* /ˈləukəl/: 1. Stammlokal, nächste Wirtschaft / Kneipe
2. (Pl.) "the locals" = "die Einheimischen"

1. The Red Lion is my **local**.

   *Der Red Lion ist mein **Stammlokal** / die **nächste Wirtschaft** / **Kneipe**.*

2. The **locals** are pretty taciturn.

   *Die **Einheimischen** sind recht wortkarg.*

E *local (adj.):* örtlich, lokal

MANAGEN / MANAGE

G *managen:* 1. (geschickt handhaben) to see to, to fix
2. (Star, Sportler) to manage

1. Das mit dem Rabatt werde ich schon **managen**.   *I'll **see to** / I'll **fix** that business with the discount.*

2. Tim **managt** jetzt die Popsängerin Plutonna.   *Tim is now **managing** the pop singer Plutonna.*

E *manage:* 1. (Unternehmen) leiten
2. gelingen, es schaffen
3. (finanziell) auskommen
4. siehe G2.

1. He **manages** our branch in Croydon.   *Er **leitet** unsere Filiale in Croydon.*

2. We **managed** to save £3000.   *Es **gelang uns**, 3000 Pfund zu sparen.*

   I don't know how he **managed** to reassure her.   *Ich weiß nicht, wie er **es geschafft hat**, sie zu beruhigen.*

3. Can she **manage** on £80 a week?   *Kann sie mit 80 Pfund pro Woche **auskommen**?*

MANDAT / MANDATE

G *Mandat:* 1. (Sitz im Parlament usw.) seat
2. (Auftrag eines Anwalts) brief
3. (Auftrag eines Abgeordneten, einer Regierungspartei) mandate

1. Aus London wird berichtet, daß die Labour-Party mit 330 **Mandaten** nunmehr die stärkste Fraktion stellt.   *It is reported from London that the Labour Party is now the strongest parliamentary party with 330 **seats**.*

2. Kein Anwalt wollte das **Mandat** übernehmen.   *No lawyer wished to take on the **brief**.*

3. Die Verstaatlichung der Stahlindustrie stand in unserem Wahlprogramm: Wir haben das **Mandat**, diese Politik umzusetzen.   *The nationalization of the steel industry was in our election manifesto: we have a **mandate** to implement this policy.*

E *mandate* /ˈmændeɪt/: siehe *nur* G3.

MARKIEREN / MARK

G *markieren:* 1. (so tun, als ob ...) to pretend
2. (sonst, auch Fußball) to mark

1. Warum muß Udo immer den Macho markieren? — *Why does Udo always have to pretend he's macho?*

2. Dieser Vertrag **markiert** einen Durchbruch in den Beziehungen unserer beiden Länder. — *This treaty **marks** a breakthrough in the relations between our two countries.*

   Die beiden Stürmer waren gut **markiert**. — *The two forwards were well **marked**.*

E *mark (v.):* 1. korrigieren; zensieren, benoten
2. siehe G2.

MEDAILLON / MEDALLION

G *Medaillon:* 1. (an einer Kette getragene Kapsel zur Aufbewahrung eines Bildes) locket /ˈlɒkɪt/
2. (sonst) medallion

1. Ich öffnete das **Medaillon** und entdeckte das Bild eines jungen Soldaten. — *I opened the **locket** and discovered the picture of a young soldier.*

2. Kalbs- / Schweine**medaillons** — ***medallions** of veal / pork*

E *medallion* /məˈdælɪən/: 1. (= medal) Medaille
2. (sonst) Medaillon (aber nicht im Sinne von G1)

MESSE / MESS

G *Messe:* 1. (Handels-) (trade) fair*
2. (relig., mus.) mass
3. (Raum für Offiziere bzw. Mannschaften) mess

1. Auf der **Messe** finde ich immer viele neue Kunden. — *I always find a lot of new customers at the **trade fair**.*

2. Gehst du jeden Sonntag zur **Messe**? — *Do you go to **mass** every Sunday?*

3. Offiziers**messe** *officers' **mess**/*
*(Schiff) **wardroom** /ˈwɔːdruːm/*

* N.B. *Fair* (oder *funfair*) bezeichnet auch eine *Kirmes*.

E *mess:* 1. vages, abwertendes Wort, das je nach Kontext Unordnung, Dreck oder eine vertrackte Situation bezeichnet: Schweinerei, Unordnung, Durcheinander, Schlamassel

   2. Messe, Kasino (für Offiziere usw.): vgl. G3.

MIMIK / MIMIC

G *Mimik:* (facial) expression, expression (on s.o.'s face)

Er mußte nichts sagen: seine ganze **Mimik** zeigte Verachtung.

He didn't have to say anything: his whole (facial) expression showed scorn.

E *mimic:* bezeichnet jmdn., der andere Leute, Tiere usw. (gut oder schlecht) imitiert: Nachahmer(in), Imitator(in); Umschreibung mit *nachahmen, nachmachen* usw.

He's a brilliant **mimic** - you should hear him doing the Prime Minister.

*Er kann andere Leute hervorragend **nachahmen** - du solltest mal hören, wie er den Premierminister imitiert.*

MINE / MINE

G *Mine:* 1. (für Kugelschreiber usw.) cartridge, refill /ˈriːfɪl/
            (für Bleistift) lead /led/
         2. (Waffe; Bergwerk) mine

1. Ich brauche eine neue **Mine** für meinen Kugelschreiber.

   *I need a new **refill** / **cartridge** for my ballpoint.*

   Die **Mine** in einem normalen Bleistift besteht aus Graphit.

   *The **lead** in a normal pencil is made of graphite.*

E *mine:* siehe G2. Wird auch im übertragenen Sinn (= Quelle) benutzt, bes. in der Redewendung *a mine of information.*

Have you ever talked to Old Ned, the fisherman? When it comes to the Dorset coast, he's **a mine of information**.	*Hast du je mit dem Fischer Old Ned gesprochen? Wenn es um die Küste von Dorset geht, ist er **eine unerschöpfliche Quelle**.*

MISERE / MISÈRE, MISERY

G *Misere:*   crisis, very bad situation, deplorable state of .... (Umschreibungen sind oft erforderlich.)

Keine Regierung scheint zu Ausgaben bereit zu sein, um die **Ausbildungsmisere** in diesem Land zu lindern.	*No government appears to be prepared to spend money to alleviate the **deplorable state of training** in this country.*
Der finanziellen **Misere** ist nicht durch weitere Kredite beizukommen.	*The financial **crisis** cannot be tackled by taking out further loans.*

E *misère:*   (bei bestimmten Whist-Spielen) Null(spiel)

E *misery:*   Elend, Kummer; Qualen

The war brought only **misery** for the civilian population.	*Für die Zivilbevölkerung brachte der Krieg nur **Elend**.*
to put an animal out of its **misery**	*ein Tier von seinen **Qualen** erlösen*

MODE / MODE

G *Mode:*   fashion

Solche bauschigen Röcke sind jetzt **Mode**.	*Full skirts like this are the **fashion** now.*
Ich weiß nicht, ob es nur **Mode** ist, wenn die Leute heutzutage weniger Fleisch essen.	*I don't know if it's just a matter of **fashion** when people eat less meat nowadays.*
Modeschmuck	***fashion** jewellery*

E *mode:* Art (und Weise), Modalität. Es gibt auch viele spezielle fachsprachliche Anwendungen des engl. Wortes.

The new **mode** of dealing with this sort of case has many advantages.

*Die neue **Art und Weise**, wie man so einen Fall behandelt, hat viele Vorteile.*

MOMENT / MOMENT

G *Moment:* 1. (das Moment) factor, element; (Physik) moment
2. (der Moment) moment

1. Ein wichtiges **Moment** bei diesen Verhandlungen ist die Frage der Inspektion der Raketenbasen.

*An important **factor / element** in these negotiations is the question of the inspection of missile bases.*

Trägheits**moment**

***moment** of inertia*

E *moment:* siehe G1 und G2. "Of great / little / such moment" (formell) drückt Wichtigkeit aus.

It was hardly the right atmosphere for decisions **of such moment**.

*Es war kaum die richtige Atmosphäre für Entscheidungen **von solcher Bedeutung**.*

SECTION F - EXERCISES

A. TRUE OR FALSE?

Mark the following sentences T or F as appropriate. Write corrections for the false sentences in the column on the right.

                                                              T   F   CORRECTION

1. Farmers cut corn in summer.
2. Hanover holds a famous annual trade mess.
3. The government is usually formed by the party which has the largest number of mandates in the House of Commons.
4. The BBC has many foreign correspondents sending up-to-date reports from abroad.
5. If you buy a holiday home abroad, you run the risk of being treated with suspicion by the locals.
6. Ballpoint pens need to have new mines fitted periodically.
7. If you need a detailed general knowledge reference work, a 25-volume lexicon is the answer.
8. Digital watches usually have an alarm clock mode and a stopwatch mode.
9. A carnival normally takes place in summer, with long processions through city streets.
10. It is usual to keep a good stock of conserves in your larder in case of emergency.
11. Army officers dine in the officers' mess.
12. Painters paint landscapes.
13. Walkers walk in the scenery.
14. Farmers work the land.
15. Statistics show that criminality is increasing in inner cities.
16. People sometimes win their legal battles at the second instance.
17. Some people simply can't be hindered from taking to a life of crime.
18. For decades now there have been all sorts of political problems in the Persian Golf.
19. 'Excursion' is a synonym for 'field trip'.
20. The dead are sometimes honoured at memorial services.

B. LAND, COUNTRY, or COUNTRYSIDE?

1. Where would you prefer to live - in town or in the .... ?
2. The sweeping views over the .... from that hill are breathtaking.
3. If they build a motorway through here, the .... will be ruined.
4. I hear Ted is buying .... in California.
5. We were stuck on our boat, and it was ages before we caught a glimpse of ....

C. FAIR, MESS, or MASS?

1. She's religious, but she rarely goes to ....
2. You'd better tidy up your room - it's in a terrible .... !
3. There's a .... in town: I saw them putting up the big wheel.
4. The lieutenant left the colonel's office and strolled over to the officers' ....
5. We're hoping to secure more orders at the next trade ....

D. DRAFT, PLAN, or CONCEPT?

1. The new .... for dealing with wage disputes has already been rejected.
2. The child seems incapable of grasping the .... of loyalty.
3. This is only the second .... - not the final version of my essay.

E. Translate the words in brackets so that they fit into the sentences:

1. His .... (Mimik) are so good that he should have become a clown.
2. We'll have to put on our mouse .... (Kostüme) for the fancy-dress ball!
3. Did you .... (managen) that business with the cheap flights?
4. Whenever we meet new people, Fred .... (markieren) he's an intellectual.
5. Do you know any good .... (Kur) for eczema?
6. The economic .... (Misere) seems to be going from bad to worse.
7. I don't feel that the future of the canteen is an important .... (Moment) in our present discussions.
8. If the children get too .... (laut), just throw them out.
9. Is your cousin Cecily still collecting...................... (Antiquitäten)?
10. We haven't allowed for expenses like that in our .... (Haushalt).
11. You'll have to ask the .... (Hausmeister) to let you in.
12. How many .... (Konzerte) did Vivaldi write?
13. They say he worked for British .... (Nachrichtendienst) in the war.
14. As a shorthand-typist who speaks French and Spanish, Ann has the right qualifications to apply for a job as a .... (Korrespondentin).

SECTION G

MONDÄN / MUNDANE

G mondän: sophisticated /sə'fɪstɪˌkeɪtɪd/, elegant, fashionable

Der Hochstapler erzielte seine größten Erfolge im **mondänen** Monte Carlo.	*The confidence trickster had his greatest successes in the **fashionable/ sophisticated/elegant** surroundings of Monte Carlo.*

E mundane /mʌn'deɪn/: alltäglich, profan, Routine-

The lawyer was tired of wasting his time with such **mundane** matters as wills and contracts of sale.	*Der Anwalt hatte es satt, sich mit solchen **Routine**sachen wie Testamenten und Kaufverträgen abzugeben.*

MONTAGE / MONTAGE

G Montage: 1. (Teil des Herstellungsprozesses) assembly
2. (Installation) installation, (bei kleineren Geräten auch) fitting
3. (Aufbau: von Gerüst usw.) erection
4. (Film: Gestaltung durch Schneiden, Auswählen usw.) editing, Umschreibung mit *to edit*
5. "auf Montage sein" = to be away on a job
6. (Kunst, Literatur; Film: Überblendungstechnik) montage

1. Die Teile werden weiterhin in Deutschland hergestellt, die **Montage** ist aber nach Spanien verlagert worden.
   *The parts are still being manufactured in Germany, but the **assembly** has been transferred to Spain.*

2. Für die **Montage** der Maschine in Ihrem Werk benötigen wir etwa zwei Tage.
   *The **installation** of the machine in your factory will take about two days.*

3. Die **Montage** der Alarmanlage ist eine Sache von einer halben Stunde.
   *The **fitting** of the alarm takes a mere half hour.*

4. Bei der **Montage** eines Films wird sehr viel Material weggeworfen.
   *A lot of material is thrown away when a film is **edited**.*

5. Nein, meinen Mann können Sie nicht sprechen - er ist **auf Montage**.
   *No, you can't speak to my husband - he's **away on a job**.*

E montage /mɒn'tɑːʒ/: siehe G6.

MOOR / MOOR

G *Moor:* bog

Machen Sie hier keine Wanderung ohne Kompaß und eine gute Landkarte: es gibt nämlich mehrere tückische **Moore** in diesem Gebiet.

*Don't go for any walks here without a compass and a good map: there are several treacherous **bogs** in this area.*

Hoch**moor**
Flach**moor**

moor
fen, marsh

E *moor* /mɔː/ *(oft im Plural: moors* /mɔːz/*):* Hoch**moor**, Heide**moor**

Ann loves to take her dog for walks on the **moor(s)**.

*Ann geht sehr gern mit ihrem Hund auf dem **Hochmoor** spazieren.*

NÄMLICH / NAMELY

G *nämlich:* 1. (um einen Kausalzusammenhang herzustellen) Umschreibung mit *because*; braucht oft nicht übersetzt zu werden, wenn der Kontext den Zusammenhang klar macht.
2. (und zwar) namely

1. Nein, ich fahre nicht in Urlaub - ich bin **nämlich** pleite.

   No, I'm not going on holiday - (because) I'm broke.

2. Er besitzt mehrere Vögel, **nämlich** zwei Papageien und vier Wellensittiche.

   *He owns several birds, **namely** two parrots and four budgerigars.*

E *namely:* siehe *nur* G2.

NOBEL / NOBLE

G *nobel:* 1. (ugs.: vornehm, luxuriös) posh, fancy
2. (ugs.: großzügig) generous
3. (edel) noble: vgl. E1.

1. In so einem **noblen** Hotel fühle ich mich nicht wohl.

   *I don't feel at ease in a **posh / fancy** hotel like this one.*

2. Das ist aber **nobel** von dir, daß du uns alle zum Essen einlädst.   It's very **generous** of you to invite us all out for a meal.

E *noble:* 1. edel(mütig)
2. adlig

1. I don't like these old tragedies with all their **noble** heroes.   Ich mag diese alten Tragödien mit all ihren **edlen** Helden nicht.
2. He comes from a **noble** family.   Er stammt aus einer **Adels**familie.

NOTORISCH / NOTORIOUS

G *notorisch:* 1. (gewohnheitsmäßig) habitual
2. (berüchtigt) notorious /nəʊˈtɔːrɪəs/

Probleme ergeben sich hier vor allem aus der Interpretation des dt. Wortes. Wenn z.B. *notorischer Trinker* jmdn. bezeichnet, der viel trinkt und dessen Problem allgemein bekannt ist, dann wäre die Übersetzung *notorious drinker* akzeptabel. Wenn aber nur jmd. gemeint ist, der gewohnheitsmäßig viel trinkt, und dessen Angewohnheit lediglich einem relativ kleinen Kreis (Familie, Freunden usw.) bekannt ist, dann wäre *notorious* falsch: *habitual drinker* oder *alcoholic* wären genauer. Auf jeden Fall ist bei der Übersetzung von *notorisch* Vorsicht geboten, und es ist zu bedenken, daß das engl. Wort *notorious* im Gegensatz zum Deutschen *notorisch* verstärkt die Bedeutung *skandalös* oder gar *infam* beinhaltet.

NOUGAT / NOUGAT

G *Nougat* / E *nougat* /ˈnuːgɑː/: Hier sind zwei verschiedene Arten von Süßwaren gemeint, für die es in der anderen Sprache jeweils keine direkte Übersetzung gibt. Das engl. *nougat* ist eine weiße Süßigkeit, die in etwa dem dt. *türkischen Honig* entspricht. Das dt. *Nougat* als Füllung für Pralinen und Tafelschokolade ist den englischen Süßigkeitsherstellern unbekannt, aber das, was in Großbritannien manchmal als *truffle* oder *praline* bezeichnet wird, ist dem dt. Produkt ähnlich.

NOVELLE / NOVEL

G *Novelle:* 1. short story, "novella". (Zwischen *Kurzgeschichte* und *Novelle* wird im Engl. normalerweise nicht unterschieden; "novella" ist ein Fachterminus aus der Literaturwissenschaft und nicht allgemein bekannt.)

2. (Gesetzesänderung, -ergänzung) amendment (to a law)

1. Die deutsche Literatur ist für ihre vielen spannenden **Novellen** bekannt.

   *German literature is well known for its many exciting **short stories** / **novellas**.*

2. Durch diese **Novelle** verliert das Gesetz an abschreckender Wirkung.

   *This **amendment** will reduce the deterrent effect of the law.*

E *novel:* Roman

Ich glaube, Jane Austen hat sechs **Romane** geschrieben.

*I think Jane Austen wrote six **novels**.*

OFFENSIV / OFFENSIVE

G *offensiv:* attacking, offensive /ə'fensɪv/ (aber siehe E *offensive!*)

Der General bediente sich immer einer **offensiven** Taktik.

*The General always used **attacking** / **offensive** tactics.*

E *offensive:* 1. ausfallend, beleidigend, anstößig
2. widerlich, abstoßend
3. offensiv (bes. mil., im Gegensatz zu *defensive*) - siehe G *offensiv*.

1. He became **offensive**.

   *Er wurde **ausfallend**.*

   "Nigger" is nowadays regarded as a highly **offensive** word.

   *"Nigger" gilt heutzutage als ein äußerst **beleidigendes** Wort.*

   They found the sex scenes in the film **offensive**.

   *Sie fanden die Sexszenen im Film **anstößig**.*

2. The stew gave off a rather **offensive** smell.

   *Ein ziemlich **abstoßender** Geruch ging von dem Eintopf aus.*

PALETTE / PALETTE

G *Palette:* 1. (Sortiment) range, variety, assortment
2. (für Transport von Dosen usw.) pallet / 'pælɪt/
3. (Platte für Farben) palette / 'pælɪt/

1. Wir führen eine breite **Palette** von Stereoanlagen.	*We stock a wide **range** of stereo systems.*
2. Wir haben ganze **Paletten** von Katzenfutter im Regen stehen, nur weil unser Gabelstapler kaputt ist.	*We've got whole **pallets** of cat food standing in the rain just because our forklift truck isn't working.*
3. Der Maler mischte etwas zerstreut seine Farben auf der **Palette**.	*The painter was rather absent-mindedly mixing his paints on the **palette**.*

E *palette:* siehe *nur* G3.

PARAGRAPH / PARAGRAPH

G *Paragraph:* (§) section; [Pl., übertr. = (bürokratische) Bestimmungen] - (rules and) regulations

Die neue Bestimmung finden Sie in **Paragraph** (§) 44.	*You'll find the new provision in **Section** 44.*
Wer blickt durch diese ganzen **Paragraphen** noch durch?	*Is there anyone who can still find his way through all these **(rules and) regulations**?*
Paragraphendickicht / -dschungel	*maze / jungle of **regulations***
Paragraphenreiter	*stickler for the **rules***

E *paragraph:* Absatz

I think this **paragraph** is too long and that it's confusing for the reader.	*Ich meine, dieser **Absatz** ist zu lang und für den Leser verwirrend.*

PAROLE / PAROLE

G *Parole:* 1. (politischer Slogan usw.) slogan /ˈsləʊgən/
2. (mil. usw.: Kennwort) password

1. Rechtsextreme Demonstranten riefen die üblichen **Parolen**.

   *Extreme right-wing demonstrators were shouting the usual **slogans**.*

2. Die **Parole** lautet "Goldammer".

   *The **password** is "Yellowhammer".*

E *parole* /pəˈrəʊl/: 1. (bei Gefangenen) Bewährung; Hafturlaub
2. (bei Kriegsgefangenen usw.) Ehrenwort

1. Hans has been released on **parole**.

   *Hans ist auf **Bewährung** entlassen worden.*

   The prisoner was given four days' **parole** when his mother died.

   *Als seine Mutter starb, bekam der Häftling vier Tage **Hafturlaub**.*

2. The officer gave his **parole** / word of honour that he wouldn't try to escape.

   *Der Offizier gab sein **Ehrenwort**, daß er nicht versuchen würde zu fliehen.*

PARTEI, PARTIE / PARTY

G *Partei:* 1. (bei Mietverhältnissen) lot of tenants; (wenn Wohnhaus aus Einzelzimmern besteht) tenant
2. (gegen jmdn.) Partei ergreifen = to take sides (against s.o.) für jmdn. Partei ergreifen = to side with s.o. / to take s.o.'s side
3. (sonst meist) party

1. Wie viele **Parteien** wohnen in diesem Haus?

   *How many **lots of tenants** are there in this block?*

2. Es war taktlos von ihm, gegen den Dekan **Partei** zu **ergreifen**.

   *It was tactless of him to **take sides** against the Dean.*

   Warum mußt du immer **für** diese Minderheiten **Partei ergreifen**?

   *Why must you always **side with** these minorities?*

3. Keine von den **Parteien** hat eine absolute Mehrheit.

   *None of the **parties** has an absolute majority.*

G *Partie:* 1. (potentielle(r) Ehegatte / -gattin) eine gute Partie = *a good catch*
2. (Tennis usw.) game
3. (Körperpartie) part
4. mit von der Partie sein
   (i) (= dabei sein) to be at, to be present (at), to be there, to be involved
   (ii) (= mitmachen) to join in, to take part

1. Lola ist eine gute **Partie** - ein bißchen langweilig vielleicht, aber steinreich.

   *Lola's a good **catch** - a bit boring, perhaps, but filthy rich.*

2. Wollen wir noch eine **Partie** Schach spielen?

   *Shall we have another **game** of chess?*

3. Auf dem Bild war nur die obere **Partie** seines Körpers zu sehen.

   *Only the upper **part** of his body was visible in the picture.*

4. Du kannst nichts ohne Gertrud machen: sie will immer **mit von der Partie sein**.

   *You can't do anything without Gertrud: she always wants **to be there**.*

   Der Ausflug nach Dänemark findet nächsten Monat statt; wenn du **mit von der Partie sein** willst, mußt du dich bis Freitag anmelden.

   *The trip to Denmark takes place next month; if you want **to take part**, you have to apply by Friday.*

E *party:* 1. (pol., jur.) Partei
2. (Feier) Party, Fete, Fest

PATENT / PATENT

G *patent:* (ugs.) (Person) great, tremendous, really good (Methode, Lösung usw.) ingenious / ınˈdʒiːnɪəs /, clever, neat

Unser neuer Fotograf ist ein **patenter** Kerl.

*Our new photographer is a **great** chap.*

Er hat eine wirklich **patente** Methode zur Lösung dieses Problems entwickelt.

*He has developed a really **ingenious** way of solving this problem.*

E *patent* /ˈpeɪtənt/ oder /ˈpætənt/: 1. offensichtlich
2. patentiert
3. patent leather = *Lackleder*

1. His **patent** incompetence soon led to his dismissal.

   *Seine **offensichtliche** Unfähigkeit führte bald zu seiner Entlassung.*

2. This new **patent** car alarm appears to be more reliable than average.

   *Diese neue **patentierte** Autoalarmanlage scheint überdurchschnittlich zuverlässig zu sein.*

PENETRANT / PENETRATING

G *penetrant:* 1. (Geschmack, Geruch) pungent /ˈpʌndʒənt/, strong, (stärker) overpowering; (selten) penetrating
2. (Person, abwertend) (ugs.) pushy; insistent, aggressive, overbearing

1. Aufgrund des **penetranten** Verwesungsgeruchs mußten wir würgen.

   *We had to retch on account of the **pungent** / **overpowering** smell of decomposition.*

2. Ich würde ihn nicht als selbstbewußt, sondern als **penetrant** bezeichnen.

   *I wouldn't describe him as self-confident, but as **pushy** / **insistent** / **overbearing**.*

E *penetrating:* 1. (Geräusch) durchdringend
2. (Blick) scharf
3. scharfsinning

1. The **penetrating** sound of the drill made any sort of work impossible.

   *Das **durchdringende** Geräusch der Bohrmaschine machte jede Art von Arbeit unmöglich.*

2. Her **penetrating** gaze made him blush.

   *Ihr **scharfer** Blick ließ ihn erröten.*

3. He has given us a **penetrating** analysis of the significance of this play.

   *Er hat uns eine **scharfsinnige** Analyse der Bedeutung dieses Stücks geliefert.*

PERLE / PEARL

G *Perle:* 1. (Holz-, Glas-, auch Schweiß-) bead
            2. (Schmuck) pearl
            3. (übertr.) pearl, gem /dʒem/

1. Diese Glas**perlen** habe ich für meine kleine Tochter gekauft.

    Schweiß**perlen**

2. Sie hat ihre **Perlen** schätzen lassen.

    künstliche **Perlen**
    Zucht**perlen**

3. Unsere neue Haushälterin ist eine wahre **Perle**.

E *pearl:* siehe G2 und G3.

Pearls of wisdom (oft ironisch)

*I bought these glass **beads** for my little daughter.*

***beads** of sweat (**not** 'sweat beads')*

*She's had her **pearls** valued.*

artificial pearls
cultured pearls

*Our new housekeeper is a real **pearl** / **gem**.*

*weise **Sprüche**, kluge **Sprüche***

PERSONELL / PERSONAL

G *personell:* (relating to) staff, staff-related, staffing; (weniger oft) personnel

Die **personellen** Probleme haben wir weitgehend gelöst.

        N.B.   das **Personal**
                  die **Personal**abteilung

*We have largely solved the **staffing** problems.*

staff, personnel /ˌpɜːsəˈnel/
personnel department

E *personal* /ˈpɜːsənəl/: persönlich

Personal problems are important for the people concerned, but often boring for other people.

        N.B.   **Personal** Manager
                  /ˈpɜːsənəl/

                   Personnel Manager
                   /ˌpɜːsəˈnel/

***Persönliche** Probleme sind für die Betroffenen wichtig, für andere aber oft langweilig.*

Privatmanager, eigene(r) Manager(in)

Personalchef(in)

PFLASTER / PLASTER

G *Pflaster:* 1. (Straßenbelag)
          (i) (Fahrbahn, aus Beton oder Asphalt) road surface
          (ii) (Kopfsteinpflaster, klein) cobblestones, cobbles
          (iii) (größere Kopfsteinpflaster bei Gehwegen) paving stones
        2. (ugs., = Ort) place
        3. (Heftpflaster) plaster, (selten) sticking plaster

1. Das **Pflaster** ist so holprig, daß man sich beim Autofahren fast den Kopf stößt.
   *The **road surface** is so bumpy that you almost hit your head against the roof when you're driving.*

Dieses **Kopfsteinpflaster** sieht zwar schön aus, kann aber zu stärkerem Reifenverschleiß führen.
   *Although these **cobblestones / cobbles** look nice, they can lead to increased tyre wear.*

Das **Pflaster** des Gehweges ist sehr uneben verlegt worden.
   *The **paving stones** in this pavement have been laid very unevenly.*

2. London war schon immer ein teures **Pflaster**.
   *London's always been an expensive **place**.*

3. Immer, wenn ich mir in den Finger schneide, kann ich kein **Pflaster** finden.
   *Whenever I cut my finger, I can't find a **plaster**.*

E *plaster:* 1. Gips (auch *plaster cast / plaster of Paris* genannt)
        2. Putz, Verputz (bei Wänden usw.)
        3. siehe G3.

He's got his leg **in plaster**   a **plaster**   **cobbles / cobblestones**

SECTION G EXERCISES

A. MOOR(S), BOG(S), or FEN(S)?

1. It's great to go for a walk on the .... in summer - I love seeing the rolling hills and all the heather in bloom.//
2. You should be careful if you go on a walking holiday down there: Dartmoor has several dangerous ....
3. Just look at these .... - great agricultural land, but as flat as a pancake!
4. There's a story that a child who got sucked down into this .... now comes back as a ghost.

B. ALL ABOUT 'PARTIE'.
Complete the following sentences with a suitable translation of the word 'Partie'.

1. Let's have one more .... of tennis before we go home.
2. I reckon Margaret is a pretty good .... for Max - he should be grateful.
3. You'll have to move - I can't quite see the upper .... of your body.
4. Sometimes Larry is a pain in the neck: he always wants to be .... (mit von der Partie).

C. YES or NO? *Answer the following questions. Where you answer "No", say why not.*

	YES	NO	WHY NOT?
1. Could 2000 books be stored on a pallet in a warehouse?			
2. Do famous pop stars usually have a personnel manager?			
3. Do people who cut their fingers put plasters on them?			
4. Can people who never stop asking questions be called 'penetrating'?			
5. Can smells be offensive?			
6. Is English nougat normally soft and brown?			
7. If Tim is well known for not telling the truth, is he a notorious liar?			
8. Is 'Tonio Kröger' a novel?			
9. Can expensive, luxurious restaurants be called 'noble'?			
10. Can prisoners be let out on parole?			
11. Do women sometimes wear glass pearls?			
12. Do jet-setting film stars lead a mundane life?			

D. OUR BLOCK OF FLATS

Choose appropriate words from the following list to fit into the story below. There are some words that you will not need.

authority	flamboyant	mark	novella	parties	pretend
beads	grins	mundane	offensive	patent	pushy
because	kit	namely	officer	pearls	putty
capacity	lack	noble	official	penetrating	section
concept	landscapes	notorious	palette	personal	short story
confectionery	leers	nougat	pallet	personnel	sophisticated
countrysides	lots of tenants	novel	paragraph	posh	tenants

Do you sometimes wonder at the range of personalities that can be assembled under one roof? Take our block of flats, for example. There are six (1).................... : four single people and two couples, making eight (2).................... in all. On the second floor we have Meryl, an extrovert fashion model who dresses in (3).................... orange and pink and who frequently goes abroad to stay in (4).................... hotels and mingle with people even better off than she is. Across the landing from her is Wetrot, a (5).................... alcoholic who ekes out a living selling secondhand cars when he's sober. He can get pretty (6)................ when he's had one over the eight. Alex, who lives on the first floor directly under Meryl, is a writer. Last year he wrote a 300-page (7)............. called "Balderdash", which was rejected by 17 publishers. It's hardly surprising: the book is not exactly brimming over with (8).................... of wisdom. But Alex is the (9).................... type; he doesn't take "No" for an answer, and keeps ringing people up and knocking on their doors even after they've rejected him. Finally he persuaded someone to publish "Balderdash". So far it's sold around 23 copies worldwide. Alex is married to Rita, a simple soul with a broad smile and few teeth. She is addicted to chocolate and (10).................... , and wears high-heeled, (11).................... leather shoes more often than is good for her.

Opposite Rita and Alex are the Lipfoots. Sid Lipfoot can't work away from home (12)............ he's physically disabled. He lost the use of his right arm eight years ago in an industrial accident, but although - according to (13).................... 379 of the Health and Safety At Work Act - he should have been able to get substantial compensation from his employer, Quickvom Sausages, his attempts to sue proved both costly and fruitless. Nowadays he spends most of his time painting (14).................... left-handed from memory. His wife Sonya bought him an enormous (15).................... for Christmas. Sonya used to be the (16).................... Officer at a large (17).................... company, but she got the sack for sampling too many of the company's chocolates and sweets every lunch hour. Now she works in a shoe shop - a somewhat more (18).......... job than the last one. Underneath the Lipfoots is the caretaker Sims, usually seen walking around with his tool (19).................... He (20).................... in a slightly artifical but amiable way whenever you pass him on the stairs.

Do I sound a little negative about my closest neighbours? Have I given you the impression that I look down on them? Please don't jump to conclusions, dear reader. Consider what they think of me. They all see me as a boring little man, full of self-importance and over-zealous in the performance of my duties. Most of them know that I am a(n) (21).................... on moths, and they think that is in keeping with my less-than-scintillating personality. So what? People like Wetrot have no (22)................ of decency or law and order anyway. I don't (23).................... to be a repressive killjoy - I *am* one. *I love* my uniform. *I enjoy* being a traffic warden.

SECTION H

PICKEL / PICKLE

G *Pickel:*   1. (auf der Haut) spot, pimple, (AmE) zit
              2. (Spitzhacke) pickaxe, pick; (Eis-) ice-axe, ice-pick

1. Sie liebte ihn - trotz seiner **Pickel**.   *She loved him - despite his **spots** / pimples.*

E *pickle:*   1. (pl. Essiggemüse) mixed Pickles
             2. Das engl. *(sweet) pickle* ist eine chutneyähnliche Mischung aus Gemüse, Gewürzen, Essig und Kräutern, die bes. zu Käse und kaltem Fleisch serviert wird. Es ist unter verschiedenen Markennamen und in diversen Geschmacksrichtungen im Handel erhältlich, wird aber auch gerne zuhause selbst zubereitet.
              3. (ugs., leicht veraltet) to be in a (bit of a) pickle = in der Klemme sitzen / stecken

PLANE / PLANE

G *Plane:*   tarpaulin /taː'pɔːlɪn/

Unter der **Plane** waren Maschinenpistolen versteckt.   *Sub-machine-guns were hidden under the **tarpaulin**.*

E *plane:*   1. (math.) Ebene
            2. Flugzeug
            3. Hobel
            4. Platane (auch: *plane-tree*)

PLASTIK / PLASTIC

G *Plastik:*   (a) *die Plastik:* (Kunst) sculpture

              (b) *das Plastik:* (Kunststoff) plastic

(a) Durch diese winzige **Plastik** wird das Bürogebäude nicht attraktiver.

*This tiny **sculpture** doesn't make the office-block any more attractive.*

E *plastic:* siehe *nur* G(b).

I really don't like eating with **plastic** cutlery / cutlery **made of plastic**.

*Mit **Plastikbesteck** zu essen, finde ich grauenhaft.*

POLITIK / POLITICS

G *Politik:*   1. (im allgemeinen Sinn, in bezug auf das ganze Tätigkeitsfeld, das mit Staatsführung, Parteienstreit usw. zu tun hat) **politics**
            2. (bestimmte(r/s) Plan, Strategie, Programm usw. (um gewisse Ziele zu erreichen) **policy**

1. Was hat ein Idealist wie er in der **Politik** zu suchen?

*What's an idealist like him doing in **politics**?*

Ich interessiere mich nicht für **Politik**.

*I'm not interested in **politics**.*

2. Die neue Finanz**politik** hat das Problem der Inflation nicht gelöst.

*The new financial **policy** has not solved the problem of inflation.*

Zu dieser Zeit war die amerikanische Außen**politik** durch Isolationismus bestimmt.

*During this period American foreign **policy** was determined by isolationism.*

Das ist eine phantasielose **Politik**.

*That is an unimaginative **policy**.*

E *politics:* siehe *nur* G1.

POMPÖS / POMPOUS

G *pompös:* grand; (negativer) grandiose /ˈgrændɪəʊs/, ostentatious /ˌɒstenˈteɪʃəs/

Das ist typisch für ihn, daß er so eine **pompöse** Villa kaufen mußte.

*It's typical of him that he had to buy an **ostentatious** villa like this one.*

E *pompous:* (bezieht sich auf Personen und ihre Art zu reden und zu schreiben, nicht auf Gebäude usw.) aufgeblasen, wichtigtuerisch, geschwollen

If only that **pompous** idiot knew how ridiculous he is!

*Wenn dieser **aufgeblasene** Idiot bloß wüßte, wie lächerlich er ist!*

I've tried to read his novels, but his style is so **pompous**.

*Ich habe versucht, seine Romane zu lesen, aber sein Stil ist so **geschwollen**.*

POTENZ / POTENCY

G *Potenz:* 1. (Stärke) power, strength, (selten) potency /ˈpəʊtənsi/
2. (math.) power
3. (sexuell) potency

1. Die wirtschaftliche **Potenz** dieses Landes spiegelt sich in seiner militärischen Übermacht wider.

    *The economic **power** of this country is reflected in its military superiority.*

2. eine Zahl in die fünfte **Potenz** erheben

    *to raise a number to the **power** (of) five.*

3. Die **Potenz** des Gigolos wurde durch seinen unmäßigen Alkoholkonsum stark beeinträchtigt.

    *The gigolo's **potency** was seriously affected by his inordinate consumption of alcohol.*

E *potency:* 1. Stärke (eines alkoholischen Getränks, einer Droge usw.)
2. siehe G1 und G3.

1. Several drivers underestimated the **potency** of the mulled wine.

    *Mehrere Autofahrer haben die **Stärke** des Glühweins unterschätzt.*

PRÄDIKAT / PREDICATE

G *Prädikat:* 1. (Auszeichnung) (quality) rating
2. (Grammatik, Logik) predicate /ˈpredɪkət/

1. Der Film erhielt das **Prädikat** "wertvoll".

    The film was awarded a high quality rating.

N.B. Dieses System der Filmbewertung existiert in Großbritannien nicht.

Qualitätswein mit **Prädikat** *"wine with **special quality rating**"*

N.B. Kein richtiges Äquivalent im Engl., obwohl die Bezeichnungen *Spätlese, Auslese* usw. mittlerweile immer gebräuchlicher werden.

2. Hans, kannst du mir bitte sagen, aus welchen Wörtern das **Prädikat** besteht?   *Hans, can you please tell me which words the **predicate** consists of?*

E *predicate:* siehe *nur* G2.

PRALINE / PRALINE

G *Praline:* chocolate

eine Schachtel **Pralinen**   *a box of **chocolates***

E *praline* /ˈprɑːliːn/: Bezeichnung für eine Art Praline, deren Füllung nuß- und karamelhaltig ist (gewisse Ähnlichkeit mit dem dt. Nougat: vgl. NOUGAT / NOUGAT, Seite 90). Kein sehr geläufiges Wort: kommt vor allem bei der Beschreibung einzelner Pralinensorten vor, bei denen der Hersteller Wert auf elegant klingende Namen legt.)

PRÄMIE / PREMIUM

G *Prämie:*   1. (zusätzliche(r) Geldbetrag, Entlohnung) bonus (payment)
                2. (Gewinn bei Lotterie usw.) (additional / extra) prize
                3. (Versicherungsbeitrag) premium /ˈpriːmiəm/

1. Bei einer solchen Arbeit sind die **Prämien** oft interessanter als das Grundgehalt.   *In this sort of work the **bonuses / bonus payments** are often more interesting than the basic wage.*

2. Bei unserer Lotterie gibt es jetzt noch mehr **Prämien**.   *There are even more **additional prizes** in our lottery now.*

E *premium:*   1. siehe G3.
                 2. to be at a premium = (sehr) gefragt sein
                 3. to put a premium on s.th. = großen Wert auf etwas legen
                 4. premium bonds = britische Staatsanleihen, die keine Dividenden oder Zinsen abwerfen, bei denen es aber Losgewinne gibt

2. These old fireplaces are **at a premium** these days.
*Diese alten Kamine sind heute **sehr gefragt**.*

3. We've always **put a premium on** in-service training.
*Wir haben schon immer **großen Wert auf** Fortbildung gelegt.*

PROBE / PROBE
PROBEN / PROBE

G *Probe:*   1. (Test) test
             2. (Stichprobe usw.) sample; spot check (siehe unten)
             3. (Bewährungszeit) probationary period, trial period
             4. (Theater) rehearsal

1. Erste **Proben** in unserem Labor haben keine Beweise für Verseuchung ergeben.
*Initial **tests** in our laboratory have not produced evidence of contamination.*

Möchten Sie vielleicht eine **Probefahrt** machen?
*Perhaps you'd like a **test drive**?*

2. Dem Meerwasser werden regelmäßig **Proben** entnommen.
***Samples** of the sea-water are taken regularly.*

Stichprobe (bei Forschung usw.)
random sample
Stichprobe (bei Verkehrskontrollen usw.)
spot check

3. Hier werden alle Vertreter zunächst **auf Probe** eingestellt, egal, wieviel Erfahrung sie haben.
*All sales representatives are taken on here **for a probationary / trial period** initially, regardless of how much experience they have.*

4. Nach der zweiten **Probe** war klar, daß die Rolle des Othello mit diesem Schauspieler fehlbesetzt war.
*After the second **rehearsal** it was clear that this actor had been miscast as Othello.*

G *proben:*   to rehearse.

E *probe:*   1. Sonde (med.; Raumfahrt usw.)
            2. (Journalistenenglisch, bes. bei Schlagzeilen) Untersuchung

1. With the aid of this **probe** we can examine the stomach lining.
*Mit dieser **Sonde** können wir die Magenschleimhaut untersuchen.*

2. Minister demands tax evasion **probe**.
*Minister verlangt eine **Untersuchung** der Steuerhinterziehung.*

E *to probe:* untersuchen, auf etwas eingehen, sondieren; Umschreibung mit *bohrende Frage, detailliert nachfragen* usw.

They don't **probe** very much in the first interview.	*Beim ersten Vorstellungsgespräch wird nicht so **detailliert nachgefragt** / werden keine **bohrenden Fragen** gestellt.*

PROFAN / PROFANE

G *profan:* 1. (weltlich, nicht religiös) secular /ˈsekjələ/, worldly
2. (alltäglich) everyday, mundane /mʌnˈdeɪn/

1. Er hört nur Messen und Oratorien und hat für **profane** Musik nichts übrig.	*He only listens to masses and oratorios and has no time for **secular** music.*
Selbst die frömmsten Mönche müssen sich gelegentlich mit **profanen** Problemen auseinandersetzen.	*Even the most pious monks have to tackle **secular / worldly** problems occasionally.*
2. "Mit solch **profanen** Angelegenheiten kann ich mich leider nicht abgeben", sagte er arrogant.	*"I'm afraid I can't concern myself with such **mundane** matters", he said arrogantly.*

E *profane* /prəˈfeɪn/: wird gelegentlich im Sinne von G1 (bes. im Gegensatz zu *sacred*) verwendet, ist aber meist stark abwertend und bedeutet *gotteslästerlich*. (*Profane language* kann auch, allerdings seltener, den Gebrauch von nicht direkt blasphemischen Kraftausdrücken bezeichnen.)

Kindly refrain from using such **profane** expressions in this church.	*Bitte benützen Sie keine solchen **gotteslästerlichen** Ausdrücke in dieser Kirche.*

PROFITIEREN / PROFIT

G *profitieren* / E *profit:* Verglichen mit dem deutschen Verb *profitieren* wird *to profit* heute in einem weniger allgemeinen Sinn verwendet und sollte am besten in jedem Kontext vermieden werden, der mit finanziellen Gewinnen nichts zu tun hat. Hier bietet *to benefit* eine idiomatischere Übersetzung.

Du würdest von einem solchen Sprachkurs bestimmt **profitieren**.	*You would certainly **benefit** from one of these language courses.*

PROMINENZ / PROMINENCE

G *Prominenz:* 1. (prominente Personen) prominent person / people, prominent figure(s), top person / people, VIPs.
2. (abstrakt) prominence, Umschreibung mit *prominent*

1. Ich habe nicht den Wunsch, zur **Prominenz** zu gehören.

   *I have no desire to be one of the **top people** / to be a **VIP**.*

   Die **Prominenz** aus der Welt der Astronomie nahm an der Tagung teil.

   *The **prominent figures** from the world of astronomy attended the conference.*

2. Er täuscht eine gewisse Schüchternheit vor, genießt aber in Wirklichkeit seine **Prominenz**.

   *He affects a certain shyness, but in fact he enjoys his **prominence** / being a **prominent figure**.*

E *prominence:*   Bekanntheit, Auffälligkeit, Prominenz: vgl. G2.

Redewendungen:

to give **prominence** to s.th.

*etwas in den **Vordergrund** stellen*

to rise / to come to **prominence**

bekannt werden

PROPER / PROPER

G *proper:* 1. (gepflegt-adrett) smart, trim
2. (ordentlich) neat, tidy, neat and tidy; (ordentlich und sauber) clean and tidy
3. (sehr präzise und akkurat) meticulous /mə'tɪkjələs/, exact
4. (ugs.) nicht ganz proper = mad, crazy

1. Ist das dein neuer Anzug? **Proper, proper!**

   *Is that your new suit? Really **smart**!*

2. Wie immer war alles ganz **proper** in Susannes Zimmer.

   *As always, everything was **neat and tidy** in Susanne's room.*

3. Wir sind mit dem neuen Maler sehr zufrieden; seine Arbeit ist **proper** und preisgünstig.

   *We're very happy with the new painter; His work is **meticulous** and inexpensive.*

4. Ihr Steuerberater ist **nicht ganz proper**.

   *Her tax adviser is **mad**.*

E *proper:* 1. richtig, regelrecht (= zufriedenstellend)
2. prim and proper = (a) (meist) prüde; (b) etepetete

1. He's not a **proper** doctor - he's just a quack. | *Er ist kein **richtiger** Arzt - er ist nur ein Quacksalber.*
2. I wouldn't fancy Bertha as a girlfriend: she's too **prim and proper**. | *Bertha möchte ich nicht zur Freundin haben: sie ist mir zu **prüde**.*

You'll have to behave yourselves at Aunt Barbara's this afternoon - she's very **prim and proper**. | *Ihr müßt euch heute nachmittag bei Tante Barbara bestens benehmen - sie ist sehr **etepetete**.*

PROTOKOLL / PROTOCOL

G *Protokoll:* 1. (schriftlich, von einer Sitzung usw.) minutes; (sehr selten) protocol;
(polizeilich) statement;
(bei Gerichtsverhandlung) record
2. (diplomatische Etikette) protocol

1. Ich schreibe gerade das **Protokoll** der letzten Sitzung. | *I'm just writing the **minutes** of the last meeting.*

Herr Weber hat bei der letzten Sitzung das **Protokoll** geführt. | *Herr Weber took / kept the **minutes** at the last meeting.*

Das **Protokoll** wurde nach diesen beiden Verhören angefertigt. | *The **statement** was prepared after these two interviews / interrogations.*

Der Augenzeuge hat das alles bei der Polizei zu **Protokoll** gegeben. | *The eye-witness made a **statement** about all that to the police.*

Das **Protokoll** der Gerichtsverhandlung ist nicht mehr auffindbar. | *The **record** of the hearing is no longer to be found.*

2. Nach 30 Jahren im Auswärtigen Dienst wußte er über die obskursten Fragen des **Protokolls** Bescheid. | *After 30 years in the foreign service he knew all about the most obscure questions of **protocol**.*

E *protocol* /ˈprəʊtəˌkɒl/: siehe G2 und (selten) G1, erstes Beispiel.

PUNKTUELL / PUNCTUAL

G *punktuell:*   1. selective(ly), in a few matters of detail, dealing with selected / certain points only
                  2. (stichprobenartig) random; punktuelle Kontrolle = spot check

1. Wir haben das Thema **punktuell** besprochen.   *We discussed the topic **in a few matters of detail** / We discussed **selected points** from the topic.*

2. **Punktuelle Kontrollen** der Fahrtenschreiber wurden durchgeführt.   ***Spot checks** were carried out on the tachographs.*

   punktuelle Promille-Tests   ***random** breath tests*

E *punctual:*   pünktlich

This train's never been **punctual**.   *Dieser Zug war noch nie **pünktlich**.*

PUPPE / PUPPET

G *Puppe:*   1. (Spielzeug) doll
             2. (Schaufenster-) dummy
             3. (beim Marionettentheater) puppet;
                die Puppen tanzen lassen: siehe Beispiele
             4. (von Insekten) pupa /ˈpjuːpə/

1. Ist das so schlimm, wenn auch dein Sohn mit **Puppen** spielt?   *Is it so terrible if your son plays with **dolls** as well?*

2. Sie war damit beschäftigt, die **Puppen** im Schaufenster anzukleiden.   *She was busy dressing the **dummies** in the shop window.*

3. Diese **Puppen** werden mit dünnen Drähten geführt.   *These **puppets** are worked with thin wires.*

   Ja, dachte er, wenn ich erst Professor bin, dann **werde ich die Puppen tanzen lassen!**   *Yes, he thought, once I'm professor **I'll be pulling the strings!** / I'll show them who's boss!*

   Heute abend **lassen wir die Puppen tanzen**: Birgit hat ihre Fahrprüfung bestanden.   ***We'll be painting the town red / We'll be living it up tonight**: Birgit's passed her driving test.*

4. Die **Puppe** dieses Schmetterlings ist ca. 3 cm lang.

*The **pupa** of this butterfly is about 3 cm. long.*

E *puppet:* Marionette (vgl. G3; auch übertr.); Puppe

The President had become a mere **puppet**.

*Der Präsident war zu einer bloßen **Marionette** geworden.*

puppet régime

Marionettenregime

glove **puppet**

Handpuppe

QUITTIEREN / QUIT

G *quittieren:*
1. (eine Zahlung durch Unterschrift bestätigen) to give a receipt for
2. (durch Unterschrift bestätigen: allgemein) to sign (for)
3. (reagieren) to react (to)
4. den Dienst quittieren: to resign one's position / to resign from one's job

1. Ich habe ihm 200 Mark gegeben, aber er hat lediglich 100 Mark **quittiert**.

   *I gave him 200 marks, but he only gave me a **receipt** for 100 marks.*

2. Der Empfänger muß links unten **quittieren**.

   *The recipient must **sign** at the bottom on the left.*

3. Er **quittierte** die Angriffe mit verachtungsvollem Schweigen.

   *He **reacted to** the attacks with a contemptuous silence.*

E *quit:*
1. (bes. AmE) aufhören
2. to give a tenant notice to quit = einem Mieter kündigen

1. Why don't you **quit** moaning?

   *Warum **hörst** du nicht **auf** zu meckern?*

2. He **gave** us four weeks' **notice to quit**.

   *Er **kündigte** uns mit einer Frist von vier Wochen.*

QUOTE / QUOTA, QUOTE

G *Quote:* 1. (Statistik) rate
2. (Kontingent, Höchstzahl usw.) quota /ˈkwəʊtə/

1. Die Arbeitslosenquote beträgt 12 Prozent. *The unemployment **rate** is 12 per cent.*

2. Für die Einwanderung gibt es strenge Quoten. *There are strict immigration **quotas**.*

E *quota:* siehe G2.

E *quote:* 1. (vb.) zitieren
2. (n., ugs.) Zitat; in quotes = in Anführungszeichen

RAFFINIERT / REFINED

G *raffiniert:* 1. (gekonnt, geschickt, ausgeklügelt usw.) clever, ingenious; (gerissen: auch) cunning
2. (stilistisch verfeinert) elegant, stylish, sophisticated
3. (verfeinert, bes. Chemie, Geol.) refined

1. Er hatte sich einen **raffinierten** Plan ausgedacht, um aus dem Gefängnis zu entkommen. *He had devised an **ingenious** plan for escaping from the prison.*

2. Sie trägt immer ganz **raffinierte** Kleidung. *She always wears very **sophisticated** clothes.*

3. **raffiniertes** Öl *refined oil*

E *refined:* 1. vornehm, kultiviert (oft leicht abwertend)
2. verfeinert, raffiniert (im Sinne von G3)

1. She thinks she's so damned **refined**, just because she went to an expensive boarding school. *Sie hält sich für so verdammt **vornehm**, bloß weil sie auf einem teuren Internat war.*

2. **refined** sugar
refined steel
*raffinierter Zucker, **Raffinade**
verfeinerter Stahl*

SECTION H - EXERCISES

A. Translate the words in brackets so that they fit into the sentences.

1. He hasn't .... (mir, quittieren) for this radio yet.
2. They don't seem to have much of a .... (Politik) on illegal immigration.
3. The new .... (Plastik) of a deer in the park is incredibly lifelike.
4. As an ex-priest, he's finding it difficult to adapt to .... (profan) duties.
5. Two shiny black limousines were waiting to pick up the .... (Prominenz).
6. The last .... (Probe) of Hamlet was a complete and utter disaster.
7. Egbert bought a large tube of cream to spread over his .... (Pickel).
8. The boss gives us a large .... (Prämie) if we produce more than 75 per week.
9. The police are carrying out .... (punktuell) breath tests on that bridge.
10. I'll chair the meeting, and Moira will take the .... (Protokoll) as usual.
11. If you exceed the daily................. (Quote) of 200 litres, the rest will be dumped.
12. That forger is so .... (raffiniert) that the police will never catch him.
13. Our accountant has got six children, so his .... (Potenz) is not in doubt.
14. The six victims of the firing squad were found covered with a .... (Plane).
15. He's such a show-off that he only buys the most .... (pompös) mansions.

B. TRUE OR FALSE? Mark the following sentences T or F. Write corrections for the false sentences in the column on the right.

	T	F	CORRECTION
1. It's enormous if you get some unexpected good news.			
2. A persuasive advert can animate you to book a holiday.			
3. You can accept a job offer as long as you haven't disposed yourself otherwise.			
4. A visit by a university geology department to a local place of interest for its rocks is called an expedition.			
5. A strict and frightening lady can be called a dragon.			
6. A fête can be an outdoor money-raising activity organised by villagers for some local good cause.			
7. Two radio stations often have very similar frequencies.			
8. Big stores employ decorators to work in shop windows.			
9. Sometimes justice isn't seen to be done in courtrooms.			
10. Troops are sometimes lined up for inspection by prominent people.			
11. A caricature is the usual word for a satirical drawing in a newspaper.			

C. SYNONYM MATCHING.
Match the words on the left with their synonyms on the right.

1. a local
2. a conserve
3. a medallion
4. a mine
5. misery
6. a carnival
7. a cure
8. to insert
9. a mandate
10. a mimic

(a) a person who is good at copying others' mannerisms
(b) a period spent for health reasons in a spa
(c) an unusual word for high-quality jam
(d) the usual word for high-quality jam
(e) a general term for tinned (AmE canned) food
(f) to put into
(g) any pub or restaurant
(h) official public support for a government or a policy, often manifested by an election victory
(i) a facial expression
(j) a large medal, often used for show or decoration
(k) extreme unhappiness and / or extreme poverty
(l) a place to extract coal, copper, tin etc.
(m) to advertise, e.g. in a local newspaper
(n) a parliamentary seat, e.g. in the House of Commons
(o) s.th. that is capable of getting rid of a disease
(p) a traditional large-scale festivity held in spring
(q) a pub close to your home
(r) a refill or lead for a pen or propelling pencil respectively
(s) a large piece of meat, usually veal or pork
(t) an unfortunate state of affairs, e.g. in education or finance
(u) a colourful summer event used to raise money for charity

D. Translate the following:

1. eins Komma fünf
2. Ich kann heute nicht konzentriert arbeiten.
3. Er ist auf Bewährung entlassen worden.
4. Die Kinder werden zu laut.
5. auf Montage sein
6. Hans möchte Konstrukteur werden.
7. Hat's mit der Reise geklappt?
8. ein Sandkorn
9. Die Kriminalitätsrate steigt.
10. Die Empfangsdame trägt immer ein schickes Kostüm.
11. Ich habe dir eine Schachtel Pralinen gekauft.
12. Ich hoffe, Sie können von diesem Kurs profitieren.

SECTION R

RAKETE / ROCKET

G *Rakete:* 1. (Waffe mit Sprengkopf, die weite Entfernungen zurücklegen kann, auch atomar) missile /ˈmɪsaɪl/
2. (Raumfahrt; kleinere Waffe mit geringerer Reichweite, von einem Raketenwerfer wie z.B. einer "Stalinorgel" abgefeuert; Feuerwerkskörper; auch übertr.) rocket

1. Eine einzige dieser **Raketen** könnte ganz Berlin zerstören.

   *A single one of these **missiles** could destroy the whole of Berlin.*

2. Mit dieser **Rakete** könnten wir den Mars erreichen.

   *We could reach Mars in this **rocket**.*

   Terroristen hatten das Dorf mit **Raketen** beschossen.

   *Terrorists had attacked the village with **rockets**.*

   Wir haben 10 **Raketen** für Silvester gekauft.

   *We've bought 10 **rockets** for New Year's Eve.*

   Mein neuer Wagen geht ab wie eine **Rakete**!

   *My new car goes like a **rocket**!*

E *rocket:* siehe G2.

RANGIEREN / RANGE

G *rangieren:* 1. (Rang einnehmen) to rank (among), to come (second, third usw.)
2. (Güterwagen usw.) to shunt

1. Dieser Fußballverein **rangiert** unter den letzten sechs.

   *This football club **ranks** among the bottom six.*

   Unsere Stadt **rangiert** leider an letzter Stelle, was die Sauberkeit des Strandes anbetrifft.

   *Unfortunately our town **comes** last as far as the cleanliness of the beach is concerned.*

2. Vierzehn Waggons mußten auf das Abstellgleis **rangiert** werden.

   *Fourteen goods waggons had to be **shunted** into the siding.*

E *range:* (from .... to ....) reichen, gehen (von .... bis ....)

The leisure facilities **range** from crazy golf to water-skiing.

*Die Freizeitmöglichkeiten **reichen** von Minigolf bis Wasserski.*

RASSE / RACE

G *Rasse:* 1. (Zucht-) breed; (Rassehund/-katze usw.) pedigree dog/cat
2. (Menschen-) race

1. Diese Hunde**rasse** ist sehr kinderlieb.   *This **breed** of dog is very good with children.*

   Ein solcher **Rassehund** kann über 4000 Mark kosten.   *This sort of **pedigree dog** can cost over 4000 marks.*

2. Mir ist es egal, welcher **Rasse** mein künftiger Schwiegersohn angehört.   *It's all the same to me what **race** my future son-in-law belongs to.*

E *race:* 1. Rennen
2. siehe G2.

1. Das **Rennen** geht über 20 Runden.   *It's a 20-lap **race**.*

REALISIEREN / REALISE

G *realisieren:* 1. (verwirklichen: Idee, Absicht usw.; auch finanziell: Gewinne usw.) to realise;
(Programm, Plan usw.: auch) to implement, carry out
2. (Fernsehen usw.) to produce

1. Seine Kindheitsträume sind endlich **realisiert** worden: er ist jetzt Premierminister.   *His childhood dreams have finally been **realised**: he's now Prime Minister.*

   Um seine Schulden zu zahlen, mußte er einige von seinen Vermögenswerten in Italien **realisieren**.   *To pay off his debts he had to **realise** some of his assets in Italy.*

2. Der Film wurde von Arne Goll **realisiert** und der Regisseur war Tim Blythe.   *The film was **produced** by Arne Goll and the director was Tim Blythe.*

E *realise:* 1. erkennen, einsehen, sich bewußt werden, bewußt sein, klar sein, begreifen
2. siehe G1.

1. Sorry to disturb you - **I didn't realise** you were working.   *Entschuldigung, daß ich Sie gestört habe - **mir war nicht bewußt**, daß Sie beim Arbeiten waren.*

| I think he does **realise** that his work will have to improve dramatically if he wants to stay with the company. | *Ich glaube, er **sieht** schon **ein**, daß seine Leistungen sich um einiges verbessern müssen, wenn er bei der Firma bleiben will.* |

REELL / REAL

G *reell:* 1. (anständig, solide: Geschäft usw.) **honest, fair, respectable;** (Angebot, Preis usw.) **fair, decent, reasonable**
2. (wirklich) **real, actual**

1. Solche Geschäftspraktiken sind kaum **reell** zu nennen.	*Such business practices can hardly be described as **honest**.*
Er unterbreitete mir ein **reelles** Angebot.	*He made me a **fair / decent** offer.*
Enthält dieser Vertrag **reelle** Bedingungen?	*Does this contract contain **fair / reasonable** conditions?*
Natürlich gibt es **reelle** Gebrauchtwagenhändler.	*Of course you can find **honest** secondhand car dealers.*
Unsere Kunden schätzen uns vor allem wegen unserer **reellen** Preise.	*Our customers have a high opinion of us above all because of our **fair** prices.*
2. Wir sehen keine **reellen** Möglichkeiten, diese Tierart vor dem Aussterben zu retten.	*We see no **real** possibilities for saving this species from extinction.*

E *real:* **wirklich, tatsächlich, echt** (vgl. G2)

REFERIEREN / REFER

G *referieren:* (wissenschaftliches Referat halten) **to give a paper;** (zusammenfassend berichten) **to give a report**

Professor Dawson **referiert** über die Dialekte Süditaliens.	*Professor Dawson is **giving a paper** on the dialects of southern Italy.*
Bei der nächsten Sitzung wird er über die Ergebnisse der jüngsten Verkehrsstudie **referieren.**	*At the next meeting he'll be **giving a report** on the findings of the latest traffic study.*

E *refer:* 1. to refer to: sich beziehen auf; (jmdn.) verweisen (auf etwas)
2. to refer to: sprechen von, erwähnen
3. (Patienten) überweisen

1. This passage **refers to** the Crusades.   Diese Stelle **bezieht sich auf** die Kreuzzüge.

    I **refer you** in this connection **to** page 83.   In diesem Zusammenhang **verweise ich Sie auf** Seite 83.

2. In his speech he **referred to** the earthquake several times.   In seiner Rede **erwähnte** er mehrmals das Erdbeben.

3. I'll have to **refer** you to an ENT specialist.   Ich muß Sie an einen HNO-Arzt **überweisen**.

REGISTER / REGISTER

G *Register:* 1. (in einem Buch) index; (Daumenregister) thumb index
2. (Orgel: Registerzug; auch übertr.) stop
3. (sonst meist) register

1. Es ist schade, daß das **Register** so unvollständig ist - sonst würde ich dieses Buch empfehlen.   It's a pity the **index** is so incomplete - otherwise I would recommend this book.

2. alle **Register** ziehen   to pull out all the **stops**

E *register:* siehe G Register.   cash register = Registrierkasse

REKLAMIEREN / RECLAIM

G *reklamieren:* to complain (about s.th.); (rückfragen) to query /ˈkwɪəri/;
               ein Faul reklamieren (Fußball usw.) = to claim a foul

Du mußt den Toaster gleich **reklamieren**, wenn er nicht richtig funktioniert.   You must **complain about** the toaster straight away if it doesn't work properly.

Er hat die schlechte Qualität **reklamiert**.   He **complained about** the poor quality.

Ich habe wegen eines fehlerhaften Kontoauszugs bei der Bank **reklamiert**.   I **complained** to the bank about a mistake on my bank statement.

Kann diese Rechnung stimmen? Da würde ich an deiner Stelle **reklamieren**.

*Can this bill be right? I'd **query** that if I were you.*

E *reclaim:* 1. (Land vom Meer) abgewinnen, abringen
2. (Geld usw.) (zurück)fordern
3. (Gepäck) abholen

1. The Dutch have **reclaimed** vast areas from the sea.

   *Die Holländer haben dem Meer riesige Flächen **abgewonnen**.*

2. I have **reclaimed** all the expenses I incurred.

   *Ich habe alle Auslagen, die ich hatte, **zurückgefordert**.*

3. He had forgotten to **reclaim** his baggage.

   *Er hatte vergessen, sein Gepäck **abzuholen**.*

RESIGNIEREN / RESIGN

G *resignieren:* Das Partizip-Adjektiv *resigniert* kann meist mit *resigned* übersetzt werden. Sonst läßt sich das Verb *resignieren* weniger zutreffend mit *to resign* übersetzen, weil sich beim engl. Verb andere Bedeutungen aufdrängen (siehe E1 - 3). Besser ist *to give up*.

Er machte bereits am Anfang der Sitzung einen **resignierten** Eindruck.

*Even at the beginning of the meeting he made a **resigned** impression.*

Du darfst bei einer solchen Schlappe nicht gleich **resignieren**.

*You mustn't **give up** as soon as you have a setback like this.*

E *resign:* 1. (Stelle) kündigen
2. (von einem Amt usw.) zurücktreten
3. to resign o.s. to s.th. = sich mit etwas abfinden

1. I'd rather **resign** than be sacked.

   *Ich ziehe es vor zu **kündigen**, anstatt gefeuert zu werden.*

2. The Prime Minister **resigned** this afternoon.

   *Heute nachmittag **ist** der Premierminister **zurückgetreten**.*

3. He has finally **resigned** himself to living in the provinces.

   *Er hat **sich** endlich **damit abgefunden**, in der Provinz zu leben.*

RESONANZ / RESONANCE

G *Resonanz:*   1. (Reaktion)   response   /rɪˈspɒns/
                2. (Physik)   resonance /ˈrezənəns/

1. Solche Appelle stießen bislang auf wenig   *Such appeals have met with little*
    Resonanz.   *response up to now.*

E *resonance:*   siehe G2. Wird auch auf die Klangfarbe der menschlichen Stimme bezogen und bedeutet etwa *voller Klang.*

RESSORT / RESORT

G *Ressort:*   (Zuständigkeitsbereich, konkret oder abstrakt) department

Frau Schiller wird nächsten Monat das   *Frau Schiller will be taking over the*
Ressort Wiederverwertung übernehmen.   *recycling* ***department*** *next month.*

Was soll ich dazu sagen? **Das fällt nicht**   *What am I supposed to say about that?*
in mein Ressort.   *It's not my department / It's got*
                                                 nothing to do with me.

E *resort* /rɪˈzɔːt/:   1. Aufenthaltsort (für Urlaub usw.)
                         2. **as a last resort / in the last resort** = wenn alle Stricke reißen, schlimmstenfalls

1. holiday resort   *Urlaubsort, Ferienort*
    seaside resort   *Seebad*
    ski resort   *Skiort*
    health resort   (auch: spa)   *Kurort*

2. **As a last resort** we can always ring   *Wenn alle Stricke reißen, können*
    up John and ask him to pick us up.   *wir immer noch John anrufen und ihn*
                                                bitten, uns abzuholen.

REVANCHIEREN (SICH) / REVENGE (O.S.)

G *sich revanchieren:*   1. (bei erlittenen Schäden, Niederlagen usw.)
                                     to get one's own back, to get one's revenge, to get even with s.o.
                            2. (um sich zu bedanken) to return the/a favour / invitation, to return s.o.'s hospitality, (formell) to reciprocate

1. Ich werde **mich** schon dafür **revanchieren**, daß er mir die Freundin ausgespannt hat.

   *Don't worry, I'll **get my own back on him** for pinching my girlfriend / I'll **get even with him** for pinching my girlfriend.*

2. Udo hat für uns sämtliche Fliesen im Badezimmer verlegt - wie können wir **uns revanchieren**?

   *Udo did all the tiling for us in the bathroom - how can we **return the favour** / how can we **reciprocate**?*

   Du hast mich gestern zu einem Eis eingeladen - jetzt möchte ich **mich revanchieren**.

   *You treated me to an ice-cream yesterday - now I'd like to **return the invitation**.*

E *to revenge o.s.:* sich rächen *To revenge oneself* klingt formell und wird relativ selten benutzt. Üblicher sind:

to get one's own back (on s.o. for s.th.)
to get one's revenge (on s.o. for s.th.)
to get even with s.o. (for s.th.)
to take revenge (on s.o. for s.th.)
to avenge s.th.

REVISION / REVISION

G *Revision:*   1. (jur.) appeal
               2. (Buchführung usw.) audit
               3. (Änderung) revision

1. Gegen dieses Urteil wurde **Revision** eingelegt.

   *An **appeal** was lodged against this verdict.*

   Hoffentlich gewinnen wir, wenn wir **in die Revision gehen**.

   *I hope we'll win if we **appeal**.*

2. Dieser illegale Geldtransfer ist bei der **Revision** aufgedeckt worden.

   *This illegal money transfer came to light during the **audit**.*

3. Eine **Revision** des Gesetzes kommt nicht in Frage.

   *A **revision** of the law is out of the question.*

   Alles spricht für eine **Revision** dieser katastrophalen Außenpolitik.

   *Everything suggests that a **revision** of this disastrous foreign policy is needed.*

E *revision:* 1. (für Prüfung) Wiederholung, Lernen; Umschreibung mit *lernen*. (Das engl. Wort impliziert immer das Lernen von bereits durchgenommenem Stoff.)
2. siehe G3.

1. I haven't started my **revision** for the Latin test. *Ich habe noch nicht angefangen, für den Lateintest zu **lernen**.*

RINDE / RIND

G *Rinde:* 1. (Baum) bark
2. (Brot) crust
3. (Käse) rind /raınd/
4. (bei bestimmten Organen, z.B. Nieren) cortex

E *rind:* 1. siehe G3.
2. (Speck)schwarte

bark   crust   rind

RUBRIK / RUBRIC

G *Rubrik:* 1. (in einer Zeitung) column, regular column, section, feature
2. (übertr.: Kategorie) category
3. (bei verschiedenen speziellen Bedeutungen, z.B. Anweisungen in liturgischen Büchern, meist) rubric

1. Die **Rubrik** "Vor 50 Jahren" ist nicht nur bei älteren Lesern beliebt. *Our **section / feature** "50 Years Ago" is not only popular with older readers.*

2. Ich glaube nicht, daß ihre Romane zur **Rubrik** Trivialliteratur gehören. *I don't think her novels fall into the **category** of light fiction.*

E *rubric* /ˈruːbrɪk/: (selten) Das Wort ist den meisten Briten (nicht Amerikanern) höchstens im Sinne von *Prüfungsanweisungen* geläufig, obwohl *examination instructions* heute üblicher ist. Vgl. G3.

SANIEREN / SANITIZE

G *sanieren:*   1. (Städteplanung usw.) to redevelop (impliziert beträchtliche Umgestaltung, mit Abriß usw.); to renovate (bei Renovierung mit Erhalt der historischen Substanz)
2. (System zeitgemäß machen) to modernise
3. (Wirtschaft: Rentabilität wiederherstellen) Umschreibungen mit *profitable* usw.
4. (Umwelt: Flüsse usw.) to clean up
5. (med.: behandeln, Wunde usw.) to treat

1. Wenn die Altstadt auf diese Weise **saniert** wird, wird sie nicht wiederzuerkennen sein.

   *If the old town is **redeveloped** in this way it will no longer be recognisable.*

   Der im Krieg stark beschädigte Palast wurde mit größter Sorgfalt **saniert.**

   *The palace, which was severely damaged in the war, was **renovated** with extreme care.*

2. Unser Steuersystem muß von Grund auf **saniert** werden.

   *Our system of taxation must be completely **modernised.***

3. Es ist noch keiner Regierung gelungen, die Bundesbahn zu **sanieren.**

   *No government has yet succeeded in making the Federal Railways a **profitable** organisation.*

4. Wir müssen alle mehr für unser Wasser bezahlen, wenn unsere verseuchten Flüsse **saniert** werden sollen.

   *We must all pay more for our water if our contaminated rivers are to be **cleaned up.***

E *sanitize:*   1. (AmE) keimfrei machen, sterilisieren. (Im BrE ist *to sterilise* üblicher.)
2. (übertr.: Bericht, Protokoll, Buch usw.) verharmlosen, entschärfen (impliziert, daß etwas an und für sich Nachdenklich-Stimmendes oder gar Brisantes als "leichte Kost" aufbereitet wird)

1. Have the sheets been **sanitized**?

   *Sind die Bettlaken **sterilisiert / keimfrei gemacht** worden?*

2. The original draft contained a lot of criticism of the government, but the published report was completely **sanitized**.

*Der erste Entwurf enthielt viel Kritik an der Regierung, aber der Bericht, der veröffentlicht wurde, war völlig **verharmlost**.*

It's the usual **sanitized** picture of married life that one finds in old Hollywood films.

*Es handelt sich um das übliche **verharmloste** Bild des Ehelebens, das man in alten Hollywood-Filmen findet.*

Siehe auch **SANIERUNG / SANITATION**, Seite 170.

SCHALE / SHELL

G *Schale:* 1. (äußere Schicht):
(hart, von Eiern, Nüssen usw.) shell
(bei Obst, Gemüse) skin, peel - siehe Tabelle unten
(von Weizenkörnern usw.) husk
2. (Schüssel) bowl
3. (Sektschale) champagne glass

E *shell:* Viele Anwendungen, darunter:
1. siehe G1.
2. Muschel (wie sie am Strand gefunden werden)
3. Panzer (von Schildkröte, Insekt usw.)
4. Haus (einer Schnecke)
5. Granate (mil.)
6. Rohbau (eines im Bau befindlichen Gebäudes);
Ruine (z.B. eines zerstörten, ausgebrannten Gebäudes)

SUMMARY CHART: SCHALE

	USE	'SHELL' IS TRUE FRIEND	'SHELL' IS FALSE FRIEND
1	von Eiern, Nüssen	shell	
2	Zitrusfrüchte; Kartoffeln, Gurken, andere Gemüsesorten		peel
3	Bananen, Äpfel, Trauben, Birnen, Pfirsiche, Aprikosen, Pflaumen, andere Früchte deren Schale besonders dünn oder weich ist		skin
4	Weizenkörner usw.		husk

Note on verbs

To shell is used for eggs, nuts and peas; *to peel* is used for all items listed in rows 2 and 3 of the chart above; *to skin* is normally used only for animals, e.g. *to skin a rabbit*.

fruit with **skin**   fruit with **peel**   **egg**shell, **nut**shell

SCHEMA / SCHEME

G *Schema:*   1. (vorgeschriebenes Muster usw.) pattern, (schriftlich auch) layout
              2. (Diagramm) diagram

1. Ihm fehlt jede Flexibilität, wenn er Entscheidungen trifft; bei ihm muß alles nach einem starren **Schema** laufen.

   *He is completely lacking in flexibility when he makes decisions; with him everything has to follow a set **pattern**.*

   Wenn Sie Ihren Lebenslauf schreiben, sollten Sie sich nach diesem **Schema** richten.

   *You should follow this **layout / pattern** when you write your c.v.*

   nach **Schema F**

   *in the **usual way** / according to the usual routine*

2. Ich habe versucht, das Problem anhand dieses **Schemas** zu veranschaulichen.

   *I have tried to illustrate the problem with the aid of this **diagram**.*

E *scheme* /skiːm/:   1. Plan, Programm
                      2. Komplott, Intrige

1. Have you read anything about this new **scheme** for saving energy?

   *Hast du irgend etwas über dieses neue Energiespar**programm** gelesen?*

2. The police uncovered a **scheme** to overthrow the President.

   *Die Polizei deckte ein(en) **Komplott** gegen den Präsidenten auf.*

SCHIKANE / CHICANERY, CHICANE

G *Schikane:*   1. (Betonung der Boshaftigkeit des/der Schikanierenden) bloody-mindedness
(Betonung der Empfindungen des/der Schikanierten) harassment; Umschreibung mit *to harass, to annoy* oder ähnlichen Verben; (ugs.) to mess s.o. about / around, to muck s.o. about / around
2. mit allen Schikanen = with all the trimmings / extras
3. (Motorsport) chicane

1. Das ist reine **Schikane** von seiten der Verwaltung!

   *That's sheer **bloody-mindedness** on the part of the administration!*

   Diese neuen Bestimmungen sind die reinste **Schikane**.

   *These new regulations are only there to **mess people around** / **annoy people**.*

   Ich habe gekündigt - ich konnte es nicht mehr aushalten, daß mein Chef mir aus reiner **Schikane** die dämlichsten Jobs gab.

   *I gave in my notice - I just couldn't stand the way my boss gave me the most stupid jobs just to **harass me** / **mess/muck me about**.*

2. Er kann sich eine Jacht **mit allen Schikanen** leisten.

   *He can afford a yacht **with all the trimmings** / **extras**.*

E *chicanery* /ʃɪ'keɪnəri/:   1. Tricks, Machenschaften, Täuschungsmanöver; (jur. auch) Rechtsverdrehung
2. Haarspalterei

1. That politician is better known for his **chicanery** than his honesty.

   *Dieser Politiker ist eher für seine **Machenschaften** als für seine Ehrlichkeit bekannt.*

2. You may call this philosophical analysis; I call it **chicanery**.

   *Du nennst dies vielleicht philosophische Analyse; für mich ist es **Haarspalterei**.*

N.B. *Chicanery* wird nicht sehr häufig benutzt; das Wort hat keine Pluralform.

E *chicane* /ʃɪ'keɪn/:   (Motorsport) Schikane

SCHIZOPHREN / SCHIZOPHRENIC

G *schizophren:* 1. illogical /ɪˈlɒdʒɪkəl/, inconsistent
                 2. absurd, ridiculous
                 3. (Psychiatrie) schizophrenic /ˌskɪtsəˈfrenɪk/

1. Für diesen Englischkurs gibt es eine Kassette für Band 1 aber nicht für Band 2? Das ist ja wohl ein bißchen **schizophren**.

    *For this English course there's a cassette for volume 1 but not volume 2? That really is a bit **illogical / inconsistent**.*

2. eine **schizophrene** Idee
eine **schizophrene** Situation

    *an **absurd** / a **ridiculous** idea*
*an **absurd** / a **ridiculous** situation*

3. Er ist eindeutig **schizophren** und braucht dringend Hilfe.

    *He's clearly **schizophrenic** and urgently needs help.*

E *schizophrenic:* siehe *nur* G3.

SCHWIMMEN / SWIM

G *schwimmen:* 1. (sich im Wasser fortbewegen) to swim
                2. (auf der Wasseroberfläche treiben, nicht sinken) to float
                3. (nicht mehr weiter wissen) to be at a loss, to be lost
                4. in Geld schwimmen = to be rolling in money

2. Siehst du die Flasche, die dort auf dem Wasser **schwimmt**?

    *Can you see the bottle **floating** on the water over there?*

3. Als wir erkannten, wie viele Probleme wir lösen mußten, kamen wir ins **Schwimmen**.

    *When we realised how many problems we had to solve, we were **at a loss**.*

4. Onkel Hans **schwimmt in Geld**.

    *Uncle Hans **is rolling in money**.*

E *swim:* siehe G1.

SECTION I - EXERCISES

A. Translate the words in brackets so that they fit into the sentences.

1. I hear that their navy is now fully equipped with Exocet .... (Raketen).
2. Professor Slander .... (referieren) about libel next week.
3. I just hope you manage to .... (realisieren) some of your ambitions soon.
4. If we don't .... (reklamieren) our TV now, we won't get a new one.
5. It's sheer .... (Schikane) that they won't let you in without a visa.
6. Whatever we do, this company can't be .... (saniert) now.
7. He's good at tenses but he .... (schwimmen) if you ask him about adverbs.
8. Surely this car company .... (rangieren) among the best in the world?
9. If you make him a(n) .... (reell) offer, he's bound to accept.
10. The Dobermann is not a(n) .... (Rasse) you can trust to be gentle.
11. You were very kind to us in Hof, so now we'd like to .... (uns revanchieren).
12. Our attempts to dissuade him have so far met with little .... (Resonanz).
13. He's been responsible for the arts .... (Rubrik) in 'The Times' for years.
14. I can't deal with that - it's not in my .... (Ressort).
15. When you type business letters, I want you to follow this .... (Schema).
16. Can you find any reference to SIMMs in the .... (Register)?
17. She always keeps her room looking very .... (proper).
18. The .... (Puppen) in shop windows look pretty funny when naked.
19. Is he still unable to differentiate between subject and .... (Prädikat)?
20. Our M.P. is fighting to get a(n) .... (Revision) of this law by next spring.

B. WHAT'S ON THE OUTSIDE?

The following words all denote the outside or edge of something. Choose appropriate words to fill the gaps in the phrases below.

bark   *peel*   *shell*
crust   *rind*   *skin*

1. orange ....
2. bacon ....
3. the .... of a tree
4. the .... of a crab
5. a banana ....
6. a .... of bread
7. the .... of a snail
8. cheese ....
9. the .... of an apple
10. tomato ....
11. egg...........................
12. the .... of a plum

C. YES OR NO?

Answer the following questions with 'Yes' or 'No'. Where you answer 'No', say why not in the column on the right.

	YES	NO	WHY NOT?

1. If a publishing company gives 10% discount to some schools, but 20% to very similar schools, could its discount policy be schizophrenic?

2. After multiple arm injuries could your arm be put in plaster?

3. Is it usual for students to buy a lexicon for reference?

4. Is it impossible for an answering machine to record a message if it's not in answering mode?

5. Can a person manage a pop group?

6. Is a declaration of war an announcement of great moment?

7. Is it a compliment to describe someone as "pompous"?

8. Could a student be patently bored?

9. Can a politician resign himself to losing his job?

10. Is a probe irrelevant in the world of medicine?

D. Translate the following:

1. *Außenpolitik*
2. *Schweißperlen*
3. *eine Stichprobe (bei Forschung)*
4. *etwas in den Vordergrund stellen*
5. *punktuelle Promille-Tests*
6. *Ich werde die Puppen tanzen lassen.*
7. *etepetete*
8. *raffinierte Kleidung*
9. *die Arbeitslosenquote*
10. *Land abgewinnen*
11. *wenn alle Stricke reißen*
12. *die wirtschaftliche Potenz*
13. *zu Protokoll geben (polizeilich)*
14. *die Altstadt sanieren*
15. *einen Film realisieren*

SECTION J

SCHWINDELN / SWINDLE

G *schwindeln:*
1. (ugs.) to tell fibs, to fib, to tell them (Euphemismus für 'to tell lies'); in direkter Rede werden oft die Umschreibungen *Come off it! / Stop telling them!* benutzt
2. mir schwindelt = I feel dizzy / giddy
3. sich (durch / in etwas) schwindeln = to wangle / con one's way (through / into s.th.)

1. Was? Nur zwei Stücke, sagst du? Ich glaube, du **schwindelst:** Du hast mindestens vier Stücke gegessen!

   *What? Only two pieces, you say? I reckon you're **telling fibs:** you've had at least four pieces! / **Come off it!** You've had at least.....*

2. Können wir jetzt vom Gipfel runtergehen? **Mir schwindelt.**

   *Can we go down from the summit now? **I feel dizzy / giddy.***

3. Nur ein Schlauberger wie Dirk könnte sich durch das Medizinstudium **schwindeln**, ohne hart zu arbeiten.

   *Only a clever customer like Dirk could **con his way** through medical school without doing any hard work.*

E *swindle:* betrügen, beschwindeln. (Es handelt sich beim engl. Verb ausschließlich um finanzielle, materielle Verluste.)

That so-called consultant **swindled** me out of £500.

*Dieser sogenannte Berater hat mich um 500 Pfund **betrogen**.*

SEMINAR / SEMINAR

G *Seminar:*
1. (Lehrveranstaltung, kleinere Tagung usw.) seminar
2. (Hochschulinstitut) department
3. (Priester-) seminary

1. Wir nahmen an dem **Seminar** über Kants *Kritik der reinen Vernunft* teil.

   *We attended the **seminar** on Kant's Critique of Pure Reason.*

   Wir wollen nächstes Jahr ein einwöchiges **Seminar** über die Probleme der Sonderschulen veranstalten.

   *Next year we want to hold a one-week **seminar** on the problems of special schools.*

2. Das **Seminar** für Germanistik finden Sie im vierten Stock.

   *You'll find the German **Department** on the fourth floor.*

3. Nach einem halben Jahr verließ er das
Priesterseminar, weil ihm die nötige
Motivation fehlte.

*He left the **seminary** after six months
since he did not feel sufficiently
motivated.*

E *seminar:* siehe G1.

SENDEN, SENDER / SEND, SENDER

G *senden:* 1. (Fernehprogramm usw. ausstrahlen) to broadcast,
(bes. Signale usw.) to transmit
2. (schicken) to send

1. Das Dritte Programm hat letzten Monat
alle Bogart-Filme **gesendet**.

*Channel 3 **broadcast** all the Bogart
films last month.*

Irgend jemand **sendet** verschlüsselte
Nachrichten.

*Someone is **transmitting** coded
messages.*

2. Beiliegend **sende** ich Ihnen meine
Bewerbungsunterlagen.

*I am **sending** you herewith my
application papers.*

G *Sender:* (Radio-, Fernseh-) station; (Anlage) transmitter

Amerikanische **Fernsehsender** haben ausführlich über die Verhandlungen berichtet.

*American **TV stations** have given
full coverage of the negotiations.*

Ich habe den feindlichen **Sender** geortet.

*I have located the enemy **transmitter**.*

E *send:* schicken - siehe G2.

E *sender:* Absender (von einem Brief usw.)

She sent the letter back to the **sender**.

*Sie schickte den Brief an den
Absender zurück.*

SIMULIEREN / SIMULATE

G *simulieren:* 1. (intrans.) to pretend to be ill, to malinger; (trans.)
to pretend to have, to feign, (selten) to simulate
2. (tech.) to simulate

1. Er war nie in seinem Leben krank - er
simuliert nur.

*He's never been ill in his life - he's
just **pretending / malingering**.*

Unsere Tochter **simuliert** immer einen Migräneanfall, wenn sie Hockey spielen soll.

*Our daughter always **pretends to have / feigns** an attack of migraine when she's supposed to play hockey.*

2. Es gelang uns nicht, in diesem Experiment den Zustand der Schwerelosigkeit zu **simulieren**.

*We did not succeed in **simulating** the condition of weightlessness in this experiment.*

E *simulate:* siehe G1 und G2.

SKURRIL / SCURRILOUS

G *skurril:*   odd, bizarre, comical, (stärker: absurd) ridiculous, absurd

Der Vertreter hatte **skurrile** Methoden, potentielle Kunden einzufangen.

*The salesman had **bizarre / odd** ways of getting potential customers.*

Mit solchen **skurrilen** Ideen ruinieren Sie uns noch.

*You'll ruin us with **absurd** ideas like that.*

E *scurrilous:*   sehr abwertend; die Bedeutung ist stark kontextabhängig: ausfallend, verleumderisch; unflätig

This **scurrilous** attack led to a court case.

*Dieser **verleumderische** Angriff führte zu einem Prozeß.*

A **scurrilous** anonymous poem appeared, dealing in detail with his sexual preferences.

*Ein **unflätiges**, anonymes Gedicht erschien, das sich ausführlich mit seinen sexuellen Vorlieben befaßte.*

SOLIDE / SOLID

G *solide:*   1. (Person) respectable, decent; (Firma) reputable
2. (stabil) sturdy, strong, well-made, well-built, (seltener) solid
3. (Kenntnisse usw.) firm, sound
4. (massiv) solid

1. Man kann seinen Lebenswandel nicht als **solide** bezeichnen.

*One cannot call his way of life **respectable**.*

Birgit ist ein **solides** Mädchen.

*Birgit's a **decent / respectable** girl.*

Wenn ich sicher wäre, daß es sich um eine **solide** Firma handelt, würde ich schon etwas Geld investieren.

*If I was sure it was a **reputable** company, I would certainly invest some money in it.*

2. Für die Wanderung am Samstag brauchst du **solides** Schuhwerk.

*You'll need a **sturdy / strong** pair of shoes for the walk on Saturday.*

Diese fränkischen Bauernhäuser sind sehr **solide**.

*These Franconian farmhouses are very **well built / sturdy / solid**.*

3. Der Kurs vermittelt **solides** Grundwissen in EDV.

*The course provides a **firm** grounding in data processing.*

Ohne **solide** grammatische Kenntnisse kommst du in keiner Fremdsprache sehr weit.

*You won't make much headway in any foreign language without a **sound** knowledge of grammar.*

4. **solider** Fels

solid rock

E *solid:* 1. massiv (siehe G4.)
2. (nicht flüssig oder gasförmig) fest, hart, hart gefroren
3. (selten, = stabil) solide - siehe G2.
4. verschiedene Redensarten - siehe Beispiele

2. This butter is frozen **solid**.

*Diese Butter ist **hart gefroren**.*

4. a **solid** vote

*eine **einstimmige** Entscheidung*

I worked for five **solid** hours.

*Ich habe fünf Stunden **ununterbrochen** gearbeitet.*

SOUUERÄN / SOUEREIGN

G *souverän:* 1. (selbstsicher-überlegen) meist kein genaues Übersetzungsäquivalent; Umschreibungen sind nötig, in denen *effortless(ly)*, *supremely well* besonders nützlich sind.
2. (unabhängig) sovereign

1. Er hat die Verhandlungen souverän **geführt**.

*He handled the negotiations **beautifully / supremely well**.*

Wir bewundern die **souveräne** Art, wie er alle Probleme angeht.

*We admire the **effortless/unruffled** way in which he tackles all problems.*

Mit einem Automatikwagen kann man auch im schlimmsten Stadtverkehr **souverän** fahren.

*With an automatic car you can remain **in complete control** / remain **completely relaxed** even in the worst urban traffic.*

Auch diese besonders schwierige Sonate spielte er ganz **souverän**.

*He played even this particularly difficult sonata quite **effortlessly**./ He **made** even this particularly difficult sonata **seem easy**.*

2. ein **souveräner** Staat

*a **sovereign** state*

E *sovereign:* siehe *nur* G2.

SOZIAL / SOCIAL

G *sozial:* 1. (gesellschaftlich: neutral) social
2. (mit positivem Werturteil: gemeinnützig usw.) kein allgemeingültiges Äquivalent: siehe Beispiele; nicht gerade sehr sozial (Benehmen) = anti-social

1. soziale Mißstände

social evils

2. Unsere Politiker denken nicht immer **sozial**.

*Our politicians do not always think in a **socially responsible** manner.*

Er ist ein wohlhabender, aber auch sehr **sozialer** Mensch.

*He's a prosperous, but also very **public-spirited** / **socially aware** person.*

Das ist **nicht** gerade sehr **sozial**, wenn du nach 23 Uhr so laut Musik hörst.

*It's (pretty) **anti-social** of you to play loud music after 11 o'clock.*

Die neue Kindergeldregelung begünstigt die Reichen und ist wirklich **nicht sozial**.

*The new child benefit regulations favour the rich and are really **socially divisive**.*

Er hat wohl seinen **sozialen Tag**.

*I suppose he **must be feeling generous**.*

E *social:* siehe G1.

SPANNER / SPANNER

G *Spanner:* 1. (für Tennischläger) press; (Schuh-) shoe-tree; (Hosen-) trouser hanger
2. (ugs.: Voyeur) peeping Tom, voyeur

E *spanner:* (Schrauben)schlüssel

a peeping Tom / voyeur   a spanner

SPEKTAKEL / SPECTACLE

G *Spektakel:* 1. (Lärm) loud noise, din, row /rau/, racket
2. (Aufheben, "Theater") fuss

1. Was ist denn das für ein **Spektakel** da draußen? — *What on earth is that **row** / **din** out there?*

2. Ein **Spektakel** ist unvermeidlich, wenn sie das erfährt - darauf kannst du Gift nehmen. — *There's bound to be a **fuss** when she finds out - you can depend on that.*

E *spectacle:* 1. (imposantes) Schauspiel
2. to make a spectacle of o.s. = sich unangenehm zur Schau stellen, sich unmöglich aufführen

1. The whole coronation was a wonderful **spectacle**. — *Die ganze Krönung war ein wunderbares **Schauspiel**.*

2. Do you have to **make a spectacle of yourself** at every party? — *Mußt du **dich** auf jeder Fete so **unmöglich aufführen**?*

SPUR / SPUR

G *Spur:* 1. (eines Tieres) track(s), trail; (übertr.) keine Spur von = no sign / no trace of
2. (bei polizeilichen Ermittlungen) (piece of) evidence, clue
3. (Fahrspur) lane

1. Wir folgten der **Spur** des Dachses. — *We followed the badger's **tracks**.*

   Er zeigte keine **Spur** von Reue. — *He showed no **sign/trace** of remorse.*

2. Am Tatort wurden keine brauchbaren **Spuren** gefunden. — *No useful **evidence** was found at the scene of the crime.*

3. Warum fährst du immer auf der linken **Spur**? — *Why do you always drive in the left-hand **lane**?*

E *spur:* 1. Ansporn, Anregung
2. (Biol.: Hahn usw.; am Stiefel) Sporn

1. This project will give the pupils a **spur** to perform better. — *Durch dieses Projekt erhalten die Schüler einen **Ansporn** zu höheren Leistungen.*

2. to win one's **spurs**. — *sich die **Sporen** verdienen*

STAPELN / STAPLE

G *stapeln:* to pile up, to stack; (sich stapeln) to pile up

Diese Stühle kann man schlecht **stapeln**. — *It's not easy to **stack** these chairs.*

Seit drei Wochen **stapeln sich** die Anträge im bestreikten Paßamt. — *Applications have been **piling up** in the strike-bound passport office.*

E *staple:* (zusammen)heften (mit Heftmaschine)

You've **stapled** Mr. Smith's photo to Mr. Brown's application. — *Du hast das Foto von Mr. Smith an den Antrag von Mr. Brown **geheftet**.*

135

He's **stacking** boxes / **piling** boxes **up**.

She's **stapling** papers together.

STAR / STAR

G *Star:* 1. (Vogel) starling
2. (Augenkrankheiten):
   grauer Star = *cataract* /ˈkætəˌrækt/
   grüner Star = *glaucoma* /glɔːˈkəʊmə/
   schwarzer Star = *amaurosis* /ˌæmɔːˈrəʊsɪs/
3. (Film-, Fernseh- usw.) star

E *star:* 1. Stern
2. siehe G3.

STICH / STITCH

G *Stich:* 1. (Insekten) sting (z.B. Wespen-), bite (z.B. Mücken-)
2. (Messer-) stab (wound); (Nadel-, Spritzen- usw.) prick
3. (Kupfer-) engraving
4. (bei Kartenspielen) trick
5. jmdn. im Stich lassen = (Maschinen / Personen) to let s.o. down; (nur Personen) to leave s.o. in the lurch
6. einen Stich haben = (Lebensmittel) to be bad / off, to have gone off; (ugs., Personen) to be mad / crazy
7. (Schmerz) sharp pain, shooting pain; (Seitenstich) stitch
8. (Nähen) stitch

1. Diese Salbe hilft bei Insekten**stichen**.   *This ointment is good for insect **bites**.*

2. Ein einziger **Messerstich** genügte, um ihn zu töten.
  *A single **stab wound** was sufficient to kill him.*

3. Was kostet dieser Kupfer**stich**?
  *How much is this copper **engraving**?*

4. Wer hat den letzten **Stich** gemacht?
  *Who took the last **trick**?*

5. Mein Auto hat mich heute früh **im Stich gelassen**.
  *My car **let me down** this morning.*

  Wie konnte er nur seine Verlobte **im Stich lassen**?
  *How on earth could he **leave** his fiancée **in the lurch**?*

6. Oh - ich glaube, die Schlagsahne **hat einen Stich**.
  *Oh - I think the whipped cream **is off / has gone off**.*

  Du darfst ihn nicht ernst nehmen - **er hat einen Stich**.
  *You mustn't take him seriously - **he's crazy**.*

7. Diese **Stiche** in der Herzgegend machen mir Angst.
  *These **shooting pains** round my heart frighten me.*

  Bereits nach zwei Runden hatte ich **Seitenstiche**.
  *I had a **stitch** after only two laps.*

8. Sie konnte mit ein paar **Stichen** den Rock flicken.
  *She was able to mend the skirt with a few **stitches**.*

Siehe auch **PROBE / PROBE** für 'Stichprobe'.

E *stitch:* 1. (Stricken) Masche; (Nähen) Stich (vgl. G8)
  2. (bei Verletzungen usw.) to have stitches = Umschreibung mit *nähen*; to remove / take out stitches = die Fäden ziehen
  3. Seitenstiche / -stechen: siehe G7.
  4. Redewendungen: to be in stitches = sich totlachen / schieflachen
    A stitch in time saves nine = Was du heute kannst besorgen, das verschiebe nicht auf morgen.

1. Damn! I've dropped a **stitch**.
  *Verdammt! Ich habe eine **Masche** fallenlassen.*

2. He had to **have stitches** after the brawl in the pub.
  *Nach der Schlägerei in der Kneipe mußte er **genäht werden**.*

4. Hast du gestern abend diesen Komiker im Fernsehen gesehen? **Ich habe mich totgelacht**.
  *Did you see that comedian last night on television? **I was in stitches**.*

STORE / STORE

G *Store:* net curtain

Wenn du keine **Stores** hast, kann ja jeder reinschauen.	*If you haven't got any **net curtains** anyone can look in.*

E *store:* 1. Vorrat
2. (auch *storeroom*) Lager, Lagerraum
3. (bes. AmE) Geschäft, Laden;
   (auch BrE) (department) store = Warenhaus, Kaufhaus

1. Every squirrel has its **store** of nuts.	*Jedes Eichhörnchen hat seinen **Vorrat** an Nüssen.*
2. I've looked in the **store** - we've run out of tea.	*Ich habe im **Lager** nachgeschaut - wir haben keinen Tee mehr.*
3. All the **stores** have their sales next week.	*In allen **Warenhäusern** ist nächste Woche Schlußverkauf.*

STUPIDE / STUPID

G *stupide:* 1. (Arbeit: stumpfsinnig) mindless, monotonous, dull, soul-destroying
2. (Person: geistig schwerfällig) stupid, moronic /mə'rɒnɪk/, slow-witted

1. Ich konnte die **stupide** Arbeit in der Konservenfabrik nicht mehr ertragen.	*I couldn't stand the **soul-destroying** work in the canning factory any longer.*
2. Der anscheinend **stupide** Zollbeamte zuckte einfach mit den Achseln.	*The apparently **moronic** customs official shrugged his shoulders.*

E *stupid:* dumm, blöd

TACHOMETER / TACHOMETER

G *Tachometer* / E *tachometer* /tæ'kɒmɪtə/: Das engl. Wort gehört zur Fachsprache und ist wohl vielen Laien unbekannt; es kann jedes Gerät zur Messung der Geschwindigkeit bezeichnen, bes. aber zur Messung der Drehzahl einer Welle. Die normalen Ausdrücke, die in bezug auf Kraftfahrzeuge verwendet werden, sind folgende:

Tachometer   *speedometer* /spiː'dɒmɪtə/

Kilometerzähler   *mil(e)ometer* /maɪ'lɒmɪtə/, *(AmE) odometer* /əʊ'dɒmɪtə/

Tageskilometerzähler   *trip mil(e)ometer, (AmE) trip odometer*

Drehzahlmesser   *rev counter*

TAKT / TACT

G *Takt:*   1. (Musik: Rhythmus, wie mit 4/4, 6/8 angegeben) time; (Rhythmus allgemein) time, beat, rhythm; (übertr., bei Fahrplänen) interval
       2. (musikalische Einheit) bar
       3. (bei Motoren) stroke
       4. (Taktgefühl) tact, tactfulness

1. Ein Walzer hat 3/4 **Takt**.   *A waltz is in 3/4 **time** / **triple time**.*

   Wir gaben den **Takt** mit den Füßen an.   *We were beating **time** with our feet.*

   Ich habe es noch nie erlebt, daß diese Band im **Takt** bleibt.   *I've never known this band to **stay in time** / **to keep time**.*

   Der Schlagzeuger ist aus dem **Takt** gekommen.   *The drummer lost the **beat** / **rhythm**.*

   Die Züge nach Ulm fahren im Zweistunden**takt**.   *Trains to Ulm leave at two-hourly **intervals**.*

2. Der Cellist hat hier 50 **Takte** Pause.   *The cellist has a 50-**bar** rest here.*

3. **Zweitakt**motor / **Zweitakter**   ***two-stroke** engine*

4. Aus **Takt** sagte er nichts über den Vorfall vom vorherigen Abend.   *Out of **tact**(fulness) he said nothing about the incident the previous evening.*

E *tact:*   siehe *nur* G 4.

TANGENTE / TANGENT

G *Tangente:* 1. (Straße) ring-road
2. (Geometrie) tangent /ˈtændʒənt/

1. Die **Tangente** wird bis zum Ende des Jahrzehnts fertiggestellt. *The **ring-road** will be finished by the end of the decade.*

E *tangent:* siehe G2. To go off at a tangent = vom Thema abkommen / abschweifen

TARIF / TARIFF

G *Tarif:* 1. (bei Gehaltsverhandlungen usw.) salary scale; siehe Liste
2. (Preis, Liste von Preisen, Gebühren usw.) tariff

1. Tarifautonomie   *free collective bargaining*

   Tarifpartner   *management and unions / employers and employees / the two sides of industry*

   Tarifverhandlungen   *pay / wage / salary negotiations*

   Tarifvertrag   *pay / wage / salary agreement*

E *tariff* /ˈtærɪf/: 1. (erhobener) Zoll
2. siehe G2.

1. The country has drastically increased all import **tariffs**.   *Das Land hat alle Einfuhrzölle drastisch erhöht.*

TERRASSE / TERRACE

G *Terrasse:* 1. (bei Häusern: gepflasterter Bereich, meist zwischen Haus und Garten) patio /ˈpætiəʊ/
2. (sonst) terrace /ˈterəs/

1. Möchtest du heute auf der **Terrasse** frühstücken?   *Would you like to have breakfast on the **patio** today?*

E *terrace:* siehe G2.

N.B. terraced house = *Reihenhaus*

TESTAMENT / TESTAMENT

G *Testament:* 1. (eines Erblassers) will (aber vgl. E1)
              2. (Bibel) testament

1. Ich weiß, ihr möchtet gerne wissen, was in meinem **Testament** steht!   *I know you'd love to know what's in my* **will**!

2. das Neue **Testament**   *the New* **Testament**

E *testament:* 1. Testament (eines Erblassers), aber nur in der feststehenden förmlichen Redewendung *"This is the last will and testament of [John Smith]"*, **mit der angeblich ein "richtiges" Testament anfängt. Das normale Wort ist** *will*.

              2. siehe G2.

SECTION J - EXERCISES

A. *Translate the words in brackets so that they fit into the sentences.*

1. He's not really ill at all - he's just .... (simulieren).
2. You couldn't by any stretch of the imagination call his lifestyle .... (solide).
3. Unfortunately our rep has just had an accident on the .... (Tangente).
4. Mildred has even got a peach tree growing in a pot on her .... (Terrasse).
5. Some professors in the English .... (Seminar) are far from fluent.
6. In my opinion it's .... (nicht sozial) if you light up a pipe indoors.
7. Our team played .... (souverän) when they won the cup.
8. The ladies' hall of residence had trouble with .... (Spanner) last term.
9. The work on the conveyor-belt was so .... (stupide) that I had to leave.
10. Is your .... (Tachometer) in miles per hour or kilometres per hour?
11. What on earth is that .... (Spektakel) in the house opposite?
12. He says he only had a cup of tea with her, but I think he's .... (schwindeln).
13. The new manager has got pretty .... (skurril) methods of persuasion.
14. It'll be enough if we .... (zusammenheften) 50 sets of these notes.
15. He left those stocks and shares to his niece in his .... (Testament).
16. It's now relatively simple to have a(n) .... (grauer Star) removed.
17. The deer .... (Spuren) were clearly visible in the snow.
18. We'll simply have to get some .... (Stores) to hang in the front window.

B. *ALL ABOUT 'STICH'*
   Choose a suitable translation of the word 'Stich' from the list below to fit in the following sentences. Use plurals where necessary.

bite	lurch	stab	stitch
engraving	prick	sting	trick

   1. This spray is quite good at easing the pain of a wasp ....
   2. That's another .... I've lost! I'm really hopeless at cards!
   3. As usual, after 22 miles of the marathon he had to give up because of a ....
   4. Bertha uses a large number of different .... in her knitting.
   5. I used to have a business partner, but he left me in the.......................
   6. That looks suspiciously like a mosquito .... to me.
   7. No fewer than 27 .... wounds were found in the victim's body.
   8. I felt the short sharp .... of the needle, and then the injection was all over.
   9. Have you seen this beautiful .... ? It's real copper.

C. FIND THE ODD COUPLE

Below is a list of 24 words or phrases, 22 of which can be made into pairs of synonyms. Write down the synonymous pairs on the right, then write the remaining two in the boxes.

avenge
be resigned
bloody-mindedness
broadcast
chicane
claim back
complain
dispatch
device in motor-racing
hand in one's notice
moan
pay s.o. back

pay
plan
reclaim
resign
salary
scheme
send
take revenge for
take revenge on s.o.
tariff
tax
transmit

The odd couple is:

D. Translate the following:

1. 3/4 Takt
2. eine Schachtel Pralinen
3. ein reelles Angebot
4. ein Schraubenschlüssel
5. ein Seminar über Kernkraftwerke
6. vom Kurs profitieren
7. in die Revision gehen
8. Wo findet die Montage dieser Autos statt?
9. Nimmst du Kondensmilch in deinem Tee?
10. ein aufgeblasener Idiot
11. ein Ansporn
12. Sie müssen ganz unten quittieren, bitte.
13. Mir schwindelt.
14. Die Bewerbungen stapeln sich.

SECTION K

TICK / TICK

G *Tick:* 1. (Marotte, Schrulle) thing, quirk /kwɜːk/
2. (Muskelzuckung) tic
3. (Augenblick) moment

1. Er hat den **Tick**, jeden Tag einen anderen Schlips zu tragen.   He's got a **thing** about wearing a different tie every day / It's a **quirk** of his to wear ....

2. Sein **Tick** ist nicht das einzige Zeichen seiner Nervosität.   His **tic** is not the only sign of his nervousness.

3. Er war einen **Tick** zu spät.   He was a **moment** too late.

E *tick:* 1. das Ticken (einer Uhr)
2. Zecke

1. Ich konnte wegen des **Tickens** der Uhr nicht einschlafen.   I couldn't fall asleep because of the **tick(ing)** of the clock.

2. Die **Zecken** können eine Hirnhautentzündung und die Lyme-Krankheit übertragen.   **Ticks** can be carriers of both meningitis and Lyme Disease.

THREE SORTS OF TICK

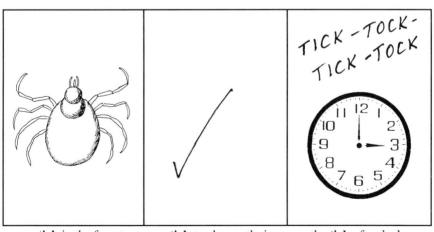

a **tick** in the forest   a **tick** to show s.th. is correct (AmE: check)   the **tick** of a clock

TORF / TURF

G *Torf:* peat; (aktuell in Irland, veraltet in Großbritannien:) turf

Bei solch einem schweren Lehmboden mußt du etwas **Torf** beimischen.
*You have to mix in some **peat** with this sort of heavy clay soil.*

E *turf:* 1. Rasen, Gras (für den gepflegten Rasen ist *lawn* üblicher)
2. (bes. bei Fertigrasen) Sode, Grassode (pl.: turfs or turves)
3. der Pferderennsport (die Bezeichnung *horse-racing* ist üblicher)

1. He spread a large cloth on the **turf**.
*Er breitete ein großes Tuch auf dem **Rasen** aus.*

2. We need another two **turfs** for this corner.
*Wir brauchen noch zwei **Soden** für diese Ecke.*

3. The **turf** has cost him a lot of money.
*Der **Pferderennsport** hat ihn viel Geld gekostet.*

turf accountant
(auch **bookmaker** genannt)
Buchmacher

TRIBUT / TRIBUTE

G *Tribut:* 1. einen hohen Tribut (an Opfern usw.) fordern = to take a heavy toll (of lives, victims, etc.)
2. (sonst meist) tribute

1. Jedes Jahr **fordert** der Nebel auf dieser Autobahnstrecke **einen hohen Tribut** an Menschenleben.
*Every year the fog on this part of the motorway **takes a heavy toll** of human lives.*

2. Jahrzehntelang mußten sie den Ägyptern **Tribut** entrichten.
*For decades they had to pay **tribute** to the Egyptians.*

Den Leistungen des Professors in der Forschung zollte der Redner den nötigen **Tribut**.
*The speaker paid due **tribute** to the professor's research achievements.*

E *tribute:* siehe G2.

TRUBEL / TROUBLE

G *Trubel:* (hustle and) bustle, hurly-burly

Silvester bleiben wir zu Hause - wir mögen den **Trubel** bei solchen Partys nicht mehr.
*We're spending New Year's Eve at home - we no longer enjoy the **hustle and bustle** of those parties.*

E *trouble:* 1. Ärger
2. Mühe
3. (Plural) Sorgen, Probleme

1. She's had a lot of **trouble** with that firm.
*Sie hatte viel **Ärger** mit dieser Firma.*

2. It's a lot of **trouble** to change banks.
*Es macht viel **Mühe**, die Bank zu wechseln.*

3. Her **troubles** were more than she could bear.
*Sie konnte ihre **Sorgen** nicht mehr ertragen.*

TUTOR(IN) / TUTOR

G *Tutor(in):* senior student giving supplementary classes to younger students

In Großbritannien werden ältere Studenten dank der strengen Regelstudienzeit so gut wie nie auf diese Weise eingesetzt. Aus diesem Grund bleiben nicht nur das Wort *tutor* - im dt. Sinne - sondern auch der bloße Begriff fast unbekannt.

E *tutor:* 1. Privatlehrer, Nachhilfelehrer
2. (Hochschule) Dozent(in). Im Hochschulwesen wird das Wort meist in Verbindung mit der Lehrveranstaltungsform *tutorial* benutzt: Hier findet eine Art Seminar / Kolloquium mit dem Dozenten / der Dozentin (*tutor*) und einer kleineren Gruppe Studenten / Studentinnen statt, oft im Anschluß an eine Vorlesung.

ÜBERSCHLAFEN / OVERSLEEP

G *überschlafen:* to sleep on (a problem, etc.)

Ich muß die Sache **überschlafen**.
*I'll have to **sleep on** it.*

E *oversleep:* zu lange schlafen, verschlafen, (ugs.) verpennen

I **overslept** and missed the linguistics lecture.	Ich habe **verschlafen** und die Linguistik-Vorlesung verpaßt.

UNVERSCHÄMT / UNASHAMED

G *unverschämt:* (Preise usw.) outrageous; (weniger oft) disgraceful, disgusting;
(Verhalten) disgraceful, disgusting;
(respektlos, frech) impertinent

Ich zahle keine acht Mark für eine Cola - das ist doch **unverschämt**!	I'm not paying eight marks for a coke - that's **outrageous**!
Es ist **unverschämt**, wie sie sich immer vordrängelt.	It's **disgraceful / disgusting** the way she's always jumping the queue.
Was heißt hier "Opa"? Seien Sie nicht **unverschämt**, junger Mann!	What do you mean, "Grandad"? Don't be **impertinent**, young man!

E *unashamed:* 1. schamlos
2. unverhohlen

1. He gave an **unashamed** account of his sexual adventures.	Er berichtete **schamlos** über seine sexuellen Abenteuer.
2. He's an **unashamed** advocate of monarchy.	Er ist ein **unverhohlener** Befürworter des Monarchismus.

URNE / URN

G *Urne:* 1. (Bei Wahlen) ballot box; zu den Urnen gehen = to go to the polls /pəʊlz/
2. (sonst) urn

1. In der **Urne** waren neben den Stimmzetteln auch einige Knöpfe.	There were some buttons in the **ballot box**, as well as the ballot papers.
2. Die Asche des Verstorbenen kommt in eine solche **Urne**.	The ashes of the dead man are put in one of these **urns**.

E *urn:* siehe G2.

N.B. tea-urn = *(große) Teemaschine (in Kantinen usw.)*

VEHIKEL / VEHICLE

G *Vehikel:* (ugs., abwertend: Auto) old banger, jalopy /dʒə'lɒpi/

Wo hast du bloß dieses **Vehikel** her?   *Where on earth did you get this old banger?*

E *vehicle:*   1. Fahrzeug (nicht abwertend!)
               2. (übertr.) Ausdrucksmittel

1. We must find out who is the owner of the **vehicle**.   *Wir müssen herausbekommen, wer der Halter des **Fahrzeugs** ist.*

2. It is a truism that language is the **vehicle** of thought.   *Es ist eine Binsenweisheit, daß die Sprache das **Ausdrucksmittel** der Gedanken ist.*

VENTILATOR / VENTILATOR

G *Ventilator:*   1. (elektrisches Gerät zur Kühlung von Räumen) fan
                  2. (sonst) ventilator /'ventɪˌleɪtə/

1. Wir mußten einen **Ventilator** fürs Büro kaufen, weil sich das Fenster nicht öffnen läßt.   *We had to buy a **fan** for the office because the window can't be opened.*

E *ventilator:*   1. Lüftungsvorrichtung, bes. aus Stahl, an einer Wand
                  2. (tech.) Gebläse, Entlüfter, Ventilator
                  3. (med.) Beatmungsgerät

a **fan**   a **ventilator**

VIRTUOS / VIRTUOUS

G *virtuos:* virtuoso /ˌvɜːtʃuˈəʊsəʊ/, masterly

Brendel spielte wie immer **virtuos**.

*As always, Brendel gave a **virtuoso** performance.*

E *virtuous* /ˈvɜːtʃuəs/: tugendhaft

Some of these monks are not quite as **virtuous** as you might think.

*Einige von diesen Mönchen sind nicht ganz so **tugendhaft**, wie Sie vielleicht denken.*

VITAL / VITAL

G *vital:* energetic, vigorous; (= äußerst wichtig) vital

Für sein Alter ist er noch recht **vital**.

*He's still very **energetic** for his age.*

E *vital:* unbedingt notwendig, unerläßlich, äußerst wichtig; lebensnotwendig

It's **vital** that you have all the locks changed.

*Es ist **unbedingt notwendig**, daß Sie alle Schlösser auswechseln lassen.*

WEIN / WINE

G *Wein:* 1. (Weinreben) vines
2. (Getränk) wine

1. Natürlich hat diese Dürre dem **Wein** geschadet - einige Reben sind völlig verdorrt.

   *Of course, this drought has harmed the **vines** - some are quite withered.*

2. Er trinkt jeden Tag eine Flasche **Wein**.

   *He drinks a bottle of **wine** every day.*

E *wine:* siehe G2.

WESTE / VEST

G *Weste:* 1. (Kleidungsstück, oft zum Anzug getragen) waistcoat, (AmE) vest
2. Zusammensetzungen: siehe Liste

1. Alle Kellner trugen schicke **Westen**. *All the waiters wore smart waistcoats.*

2. kugelsichere **Weste** *bullet-proof jacket*
Schwimm**weste** *life jacket, (AmE) life vest*
Strick**weste** *sleeveless cardigan*

E *vest:* 1. (BrE) Unterhemd
2. (AmE) Weste

1. It's not exactly nice when you turn up for dinner in that old **vest**! *Es ist nicht gerade schön, wenn du in diesem alten **Unterhemd** zum Abendessen erscheinst!*

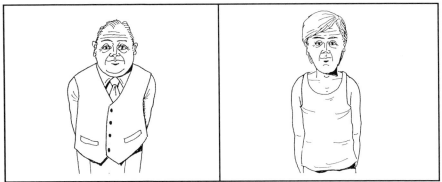

a **waistcoat**   a **vest**
(AmE: a vest)

ZENSUR / CENSURE

G *Zensur:* 1. (Kontrolle von Büchern usw.) (abstrakt) censorship, (Prüfstelle) the censors /ˈsensəz/
2. (Note) mark, grade

1. Bist du wirklich gegen jede Art von **Zensur**? *Are you really against any form of censorship?*

Der Film ist nicht durch die **Zensur** gegangen. *The film didn't get past **the censors**.*

2. Seine **Zensuren** zeigen, daß er sich am Riemen gerissen hat.

*His **marks / grades** show that he's pulled his socks up.*

E *censure* /'senʃə/: (formell) **Tadel**

He incurred great **censure** by behaving in this way.

*Durch dieses Verhalten zog er sich schweren **Tadel** zu.*

ZINN / TIN

G *Zinn:* 1. (Rohstoff, Metall) tin
2. (Legierung aus Zinn, Blei und gelegentlich auch Kupfer und Antimon) pewter
(aber: Zinnsoldat = tin soldier)

E *tin:* 1. Dose, Büchse
2. siehe G1.

ZITIEREN / CITE

G *zitieren:* 1. (vor den Schulleiter u.ä.) to summon
2. (aus einem Gedicht u.ä.; ein Beispiel) to quote, (weniger üblich) to cite

1. Der Junge wurde vor den Schulleiter **zitiert**.

*The boy was **summoned** to appear before the Head Teacher.*

Er wurde in das Büro des Personalleiters **zitiert**.

*He was **summoned** to the office of the Personnel Manager.*

2. Dauernd **zitiert** er aus Goethes Faust.

*He's forever **quoting** from Goethe's Faust.*

Ich kann mehrere Beispiele **zitieren**.

*I can **quote** several examples.*

E *cite:* 1. (bei Scheidungsprozessen) nennen - aber eine Umschreibung mit *Scheidungsgrund* ist vorzuziehen.
2. siehe G2.

1. Janis **was cited** as co-respondent in Barbara's divorce proceedings.

*Janis war der Scheidungsgrund / wurde als Mitbeklagte in Barbaras Scheidungsprozeß **genannt**.*

ZIVIL / CIVIL

G *zivil:* 1. (nicht militärisch) civilian; (bei bestimmten Kombinationen) civil (siehe Liste)
2. (Preise usw.) reasonable

1. Der Soldat freute sich auf seine Entlassung ins **Zivil**leben.

   *The soldier was looking forward to his discharge into **civilian** life.*

   Kann es jemals so etwas wie eine **zivile** Armee geben?

   *Can there ever be such a thing as a **civilian** army?*

Zivilbevölkerung	*civilian population*
Zivilbehörden	*civil authorities*
ziviler Bevölkerungsschutz / Zivilschutz	*civil defence*
Zivilcourage	*the courage of one's convictions / the courage to stand up for what one believes in*
Zivildienst (für Kriegsdienstverweigerer)	*community service (for conscientious objectors)*
Zivilehe	*civil marriage*
Zivilkleidung	*civilian clothes, (ugs.) "civvies"*
Zivilleben	*civilian life*
Zivilluftfahrt	*civil aviation*
Zivilrecht	*civil law*
ziviler Ungehorsam	*civil disobedience*

2. Im 'Roten Hahn' sind die Preise ganz **zivil**.

   *The prices at the 'Roter Hahn' are perfectly **reasonable**.*

E *civil:* 1. höflich
2. siehe G1; andere Kombinationen: siehe Liste

1. That wasn't very **civil** of you.

   *Das war nicht sehr **höflich** von dir.*

2. civil engineer — *Bauingenieur*
   civil engineering — *Bauingenieurwesen, Hoch- und Tiefbau*

   civil rights — *Bürgerrechte*
   civil servant — *Beamter, Beamtin*
   civil service — *Staatsdienst*
   civil war — *Bürgerkrieg*

SECTION K - EXERCISES

A. TRUE OR FALSE? Write T or F in the appropriate column. Write corrections for the false sentences on the right.

	T	F	CORRECTION
1. Sudden, jerky, unpredictable movements of the head are often a sign that a person has a tick.			
2. People moving into a brand new house might have to lay turves in their garden.			
3. A three-piece suit includes a vest.			
4. Pewter is not an alloy.			
5. Ventilators can help you keep cool by blowing cool air around a room.			
6. A lorry, a bus and a car are all vehicles.			
7. Tutors give lessons at British universities.			
8. A boy who is not ashamed of attacking an old lady can be said to be unashamed of that crime.			
9. When it's time to elect a new government, people go to the urns.			
10. A virtuoso person is someone with few or no vices.			
11. Politicians often pay tribute to colleagues who have just died.			
12. Wine is made from grapes, which grow on vines.			
13. You can censure an erotic film and censor a naughty child.			
14. Sometimes several lovers' names are cited in divorce cases.			
15. When off duty, soldiers often wear civil clothes.			
16. Songs often have five or six verses plus a chore which is repeated.			

B. Match the words on the left with their synonyms on the right.

a. tact (1) full of virtue
b. scurrilous (2) essential
c. virtuous (3) pickle
d. vital (4) time
e. solid (5) pile up
f. pimple (6) spot
g. staple (7) rhythm
  (8) virtual
  (9) obscenely abusive; containing obscene humour
  (10) lively
  (11) massive
  (12) virtuoso
  (13) bizarre or ridiculous
  (14) upright and respectable
  (15) diplomacy
  (16) not hollow
  (17) fasten together

C. Translate the following:

1. Das fordert einen hohen Tribut.
2. An Weihnachten herrscht großer Trubel im Zentrum.
3. Hast du verschlafen?
4. Möchtest du das Problem überschlafen?
5. Ist dieser Krug aus purem Zinn?
6. Sie leidet an grünem Star.
7. Er macht gerade Zivildienst.
8. Trägt er eigentlich ein Unterhemd unter seiner Weste?
9. Immer mußt du Shakespeare zitieren!
10. Zwanzig Mark für so eine Dose? Das ist ja unverschämt!

SECTION L - SHORT ENTRIES

| ACHSEL /
AXLE | G | **Achsel:** | shoulder |
| | E | **axle:** | die Achse |

ADRESSBUCH /
ADDRESS BOOK

G **Adreßbuch:** 1. directory (of a town / city)
2. address book (private)
E **address book:** Adreßbuch - *nur* G2.

AGIL /
AGILE

G **agil:** 1. (physically) agile /ˈædʒaɪl/
2. mentally agile, quick-witted, sharp
E **agile** /ˈædʒaɪl/: immer G1 - es sei denn, das Wort *mentally* wird vorangestellt.

AGONIE /
AGONY

G **Agonie:** death throes / agony; (selten) agony
E **agony** /ˈægəni/: 1. starke Schmerzen, Leid, Qual
2. Agonie

ALKOHOLIKA /
ALCOHOLICS

G **Alkoholika:** alcoholic drinks, alcohol
E **alcoholics:** Alkoholiker(innen)

ANGINA /
ANGINA

G **Angina:** 1. sore throat
2. (= Angina pectoris) angina
E **angina** /ænˈdʒaɪnə/: Angina - aber *nur* G2.

APPELL /
APPEAL

G **Appell:** 1.(mil.) roll-call 2. appeal
E **appeal:** Aufruf, Appell; (attraction) appeal

ARGUMENT /
ARGUMENT

G **Argument:** (Rechtfertigungsgrund) argument
E **argument:** 1. Auseinandersetzung, Streit
2. das Argumentieren
3. das Argument

| ARMBAND / ARMBAND | G | **Armband:** | bracelet; watch-strap |
| | E | **armband:** | Armbinde |

AROMA / AROMA	G	**Aroma:**	1. (Geschmack) taste, flavour
			2. (würziger Duft) aroma
			3. (Geschmacksstoff, Essenz) flavouring, essence, z.B. 'almond flavouring', 'essence of almonds'.
	E	**aroma** /ə'rəʊmə/:	siehe *nur* G2.

| ARSEN / ARSON | G | **Arsen:** | arsenic /'ɑːsnɪk/ |
| | E | **arson** /'ɑːsn/: | Brandstiftung |

AUTOMAT / AUTOMAT	G	**Automat:**	1. (Zigaretten- usw.) (vending-) machine, slot-machine, (selten) automat
			2. (Spielautomat) slot-machine, fruit-machine, one-armed bandit
	E	**automat:**	(AmE) Automatenrestaurant

| BAGGER / BUGGER | G | **Bagger:** | JCB (the initials of the company 'J.C.Bamforth'. As with *hoover* and *sellotape*, this firm has come to symbolize all products of the type); excavator, digger; (für Schlamm) dredger |
| | E | **bugger:** | 1. Sodomit 2. (ugs.) (Scheiß)kerl |

BISKUIT / BISCUIT	G	**Biskuit:**	(cul.) sponge
		Biskuitkuchen:	sponge (cake)
		Löffelbiskuit:	sponge finger
	E	**biscuit** /'bɪskɪt/:	Keks

a **sponge** (cake)   **biscuits**

BLAUÄUGIG / **BLUE-EYED**	G blauäugig:	1. (wörtlich) blue-eyed 2. (übertr.) starry-eyed, naïve
	E blue-eyed:	1. blauäugig - siehe G1. 2. his / her blue-eyed boy = sein / ihr Lieblingsjunge

BLOCK /
 BLOCK
	G Block:	1. (meist) block
		   Wohnblock = block of flats, (AmE) apartment house
		 2. Notizblock = note-pad
		   Schreibblock = writing-pad

	E block:	1. (meist) Block 2. tower block = Hochhaus

BLUBBERN / **BLUBBER**	G blubbern:	1. (ugs.) to bubble 2. (reden) to mutter, mumble, murmur
	E blubber:	(ugs.) jammern, heulen, plärren

CHRIST / **CHRIST**	G Christ:	1. Christian 2. Christ
	E Christ:	der Christus

CHRISTENTUM / **CHRISTENDOM**	G Christentum:	Christianity
	E Christendom /ˈkrɪsndəm/:	Christenheit

DEFILIEREN / **DEFILE**	G defilieren:	to march past, file past
	E defile /dɪˈfaɪl/:	schänden, entweihen, beschmutzen

DEGRADIEREN / **DEGRADE**	G degradieren:	(mil.) to demote
	E degrade s.o.:	jmdn. erniedrigen

DEPOT / **DEPOT**	G Depot:	1. (meist, für Busse usw.) depot 2. (in einer Bank) vault, strong room 3. (Schließfach) safety deposit box
	E depot /ˈdepəʊ/:	Depot, aber *nicht* G2 oder G3.

157

| DESINTERESSE /
DISINTEREST | G
E | Desinteresse:
disinterest: | total lack of interest
(Neutralität) Unparteilichkeit,
Unvoreingenommenheit;
(Apathie) Gleichgültigkeit |

| DESINTERESSIERT /
DISINTERESTED | G
E | desinteressiert:
disinterested: | uninterested, bored
(neutral) unvoreingenommen,
unparteiisch; (apathisch)
gleichgültig |

DEVISEN /   G Devisen: foreign currency, foreign exchange
DEVICE(S)   E device: 1. Gerät, Vorrichtung
                                2. literary device = ein literarischer
                                   Kunstgriff
                                3. nuclear device = ein atomarer
                                   Sprengkörper

DIAGONAL /   G diagonal: 1. (bei Linien) diagonal
DIAGONAL   2. diagonal lesen = to skim through,
                                   to flick through
                                Diagonalreifen = cross-ply tyres
                   E diagonal / daɪ'ægənl /: siehe nur G1.

DOGGE /   G Dogge: (englische) Dogge = mastiff
DOG   deutsche Dogge = Great Dane
                   E dog: Hund

DRACHENFLIEGER /   G Drachenflieger: hang-glider (pilot)
DRAGONFLY   E dragonfly: Libelle

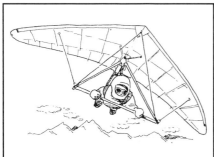 

a **hang-glider**   a **dragonfly**

See also DRACHE(N) / DRAGON, p.34

EFFEKTEN /	G	**Effekten:**	1. (fin.) stocks and shares, bonds
EFFECTS			2. (veraltet) personal effects, property
	E	**effects:**	Auswirkungen, Effekte

EXALTIERT /	G	**exaltiert:**	(Benehmen) exaggerated, effusive, over the top
EXALTED	E	**exalted:**	(Stelle) hoch; (Thema, Stil) erhaben

EXPERTISE /	G	**Expertise:**	expert's appraisal / report / opinion
EXPERTISE	E	**expertise** /ˌeksp ɜː'tiːz/:	1. Fachkenntnisse
			2. (handwerkliches) Geschick

FINALE /	G	**Finale:**	1. (mus., Schau, Zirkus u.ä.) finale
FINALE			2. (Fußball usw.) final
			Halbfinale: semi-final
	E	**finale** /fɪ'nɑːli/:	Finale - *nur* G1.

FLATTERN /	G	**flattern:**	(meist) to flutter; (Fahne, Flügel, Segel auch:) to flap
FLATTER			ins Haus flattern (Brief usw.) = to turn up at one's house
	E	**flatter:**	schmeicheln

FLICKEN /	G	**flicken:**	to mend, (Socken auch:) to darn
FLICK	E	**flick:**	(weg)schnipsen, (weg)wedeln, schnalzen

FLINTE /	G	**Flinte:**	shotgun
FLINT			die Flinte ins Korn werfen = to throw in the towel / sponge
	E	**flint:**	Feuerstein

FUSION /	G	**Fusion:**	1. (von Firmen usw.) merger, amalgamation
FUSION			2. (Kernphysik, Biologie) fusion
	E	**fusion:**	1. Verschmelzung
			2. siehe G2.

GARAGE /	G	Garage:	garage
GARAGE			Tiefgarage = underground car park
	E	garage / 'gærɑːʒ/:	1. Garage
			2. Werkstatt

GASTHAUS /	G	Gasthaus:	inn; pub (with restaurant and
GUEST-HOUSE			accommodation)
	E	guest-house:	Pension

GASTRONOMIE /	G	Gastronomie:	1. (Gewerbe) catering (trade)
GASTRONOMY			2. (gute Küche) gastronomy,
			haute cuisine
	E	gastronomy:	siehe *nur* G2.

GENIE /	G	Genie:	genius
GENIE	E	genie / 'dʒiːni/:	dienstbarer Geist; Flaschengeist

GRATIFIKATION /	G	Gratifikation:	bonus
GRATIFICATION	E	gratification:	1. Genugtuung
			2. Befriedigung
			sexual gratification = sexuelle
			Befriedigung

GURGELN /	G	gurgeln:	to gargle
GURGLE	E	gurgle:	1. (Flüssigkeit) gluckern, plätschern
			2. (Baby) glucksen

a man **gargling**   water **gurgling**

HAUSHÄLTER(IN) / HOUSEHOLDER	G Haushälter(in):	housekeeper
	E householder:	(Haus)bewohner, Hauseigentümer, Wohnungseigentümer

HELM / HELM	G Helm:	helmet Sturzhelm = crash helmet Stahlhelm = steel helmet Schutzhelm = safety helmet; (Baustelle) hard hat
	E helm:	1. Steuer, Ruder (auch übertr.) 2. (poetisch, veraltet) Helm

HERING / HERRING	G Hering:	1. herring 2. tent peg
	E herring:	Hering - *nur* G1.

HISSEN / HISS	G hissen:	to hoist, raise
	E hiss:	zischen

HYMNE / HYMN	G Hymne:	hymn. Aber *Nationalhymne* = national anthem
	E hymn:	Hymne. Aber auch die übliche Bezeichnung für *Kirchenlied*

INVALIDITÄT / INVALIDITY	G Invalidität:	disability
	E invalidity:	Ungültigkeit invalidity pension = Invaliditätsrente

JALOUSIE / JEALOUSY	G Jalousie:	(venetian) blind
	E jealousy:	Eifersucht

KAPELLE / CHAPEL	G	Kapelle:	1. (mus.) (dance-)band, group 2. (relig.) chapel
	E	chapel:	Kapelle - *nur* G2.
KASINO / CASINO	G	Kasino:	1. (Spielbank) casino 2. (Speiseraum, mil.) (officers') mess; (geh., in Firmen usw.: Speiseraum für leitende Angestellte) dining room
	E	casino /kə'siːnəʊ/:	Kasino - nur G1.
KASSETTE / CASSETTE	G	Kassette:	1. (meist) cassette 2. (für Wertsachen) box, cash-box 3. (Bücher usw.) boxed set
	E	cassette:	Kassette - nur G1.
KIPPEN / KIP	G	kippen:	(Abfall) to tip; (Fenster) to tilt
	E	kip:	(ugs.) pennen
KIPPER / KIPPER	G	Kipper:	tipper, (AmE) dump truck
	E	kipper:	geräucherter Hering, Räucherhering
KLOSTER / CLOISTER(S)	G	Kloster:	(für Männer) monastery, (für Frauen) nunnery
	E	cloister(s):	Kreuzgang

a **monastery**

cloisters

KOMMODE / COMMODE	G Kommode:	chest of drawers; (BrE veraltet; meist AmE) commode
	E commode:	Nachtstuhl; (veraltet) Kommode

 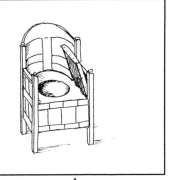

a **chest of drawers** a **commode**

KONFESSION / CONFESSION	G Konfession:	denomination, religion
	E confession:	1. (eines Verbrechens) Geständnis
		2. (relig.) Beichte

KONSTELLATION / CONSTELLATION	G Konstellation:	1. (Gesamtlage) situation
		2. (Sternbild) constellation
	E constellation:	Sternbild

KONZERN / CONCERN	G Konzern:	group, group of companies, combine /ˈkɒmbaɪn/
	E concern:	1. Firma, Unternehmen
		2. Sorge, Besorgnis
		Her condition is giving cause for concern = Ihr Zustand gibt Anlaß zu Besorgnis.
		3. Angelegenheit

KONZESSION / CONCESSION	G Konzession:	1. (für Taxifahrer usw.) licence
		2. (Zugeständnis) concession
	E concession:	1. Konzession, Einräumung
		2. (sehr selten, Wirtsch.) Konzession (G1).

163

KOTELETTEN /	G	Koteletten:	sideboards, sideburns
CUTLETS	E	cutlets:	Koteletts
			(Aber das Wort *chop* ist viel
			gebräuchlicher als *cutlet.*)

KRABBE /	G	Krabbe:	1. (ugs., kleine Garnele) shrimp
CRAB			2. (ugs., größere Garnele) prawn
			3. (Zool.) crab
	E	crab:	(Meerestier, meist) Krebs;
			(Zool.) Krabbe
			N.B. Krebs (Krankheit) = cancer

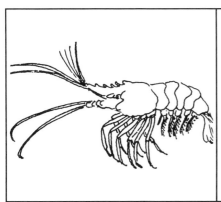
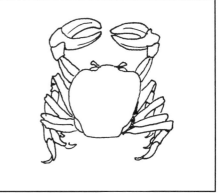

a **prawn**   a **crab**

| KURSBUCH / | G | Kursbuch: | (railway) timetable (book) |
| COURSEBOOK | E | coursebook: | Lehrbuch |

LIBELLE /	G	Libelle:	1. (Zool.) dragonfly
LIBEL			2. (tech., Wasserwaage) spirit level
	E	libel / 'laɪbəl/:	(schriftliche) Verleumdung
			N.B. mündliche Verleumdung =
			slander

See also **DRACHENFLIEGER / DRAGONFLY**, p.157.

LIMONE /	G	Limone:	lime
LEMON	E	lemon:	Zitrone

a lime   a lemon

LIQUIDE /	G	liquide:	(fin.) liquid, (Personen) solvent
LIQUID	E	liquid:	(meist) flüssig; (fin.:) liquid assets = flüssige Mittel, verfügbare Mittel

MANIFEST /	G	Manifest:	manifesto
MANIFEST	E	manifest:	Ladeverzeichnis, Frachtgutliste, (Schiffs)manifest

MARINE /	G	Marine:	navy; a marine in the merchant navy
MARINE	E	marine:	Marineinfanterist the marines = die Marineinfanterie

MELONE /	G	Melone:	1. (Frucht) melon 2. (Hut) bowler (hat)
MELON	E	melon:	siehe *nur* G1.

MILAN /	G	Milan:	(orn.) kite
MILAN	E	Milan:	Mailand

MILD /	G	mild:	1. (Wetter, Curry, Seife usw.) mild; 2. (Strafe, Bestrafung) lenient
MILD	E	mild:	siehe *nur* G1.

MOORHUHN / MOORHEN	G E	Moorhuhn: moorhen:	grouse Teichhuhn

MOTIV / MOTIVE	G	Motiv:	1. (Thema) subject, theme; (mus., Design, lit.: auch) motif 2. (Beweggrund) motive
	E	motive:	siehe *nur* G2.

MOTOR / MOTOR	G	Motor:	1. (bei Fahrzeugen) engine 2. (übertr., für Personen) driving force 3. (sonst) motor
	E	motor:	1. (bei Maschinen, Küchengeräten usw.) Motor 2. (ugs.) Auto

MUSCHEL / MUSCLE, MUSSEL	G	Muschel:	1. (leer, am Strand) shell, sea shell 2. (= Miesmuschel) mussel 3. Ohrmuschel = earpiece Sprechmuschel = mouthpiece
	E	muscle /'mʌsl/:	Muskel
	E	mussel /'mʌsl/:	Miesmuschel

NACKEN / NECK	G E	Nacken: neck:	nape (of the neck), back of the neck Hals

NAGEN / NAG	G E	nagen: nag (s.o.):	to gnaw Nagetier = rodent (an jmdm. herum)nörgeln, (an jmdm. herum)meckern

NECKEN / NECK	G E	necken: neck (ugs.):	to tease schmusen, knutschen

NEKTAR / NECTAR	G	Nektar:	1. (Bot., Myth.) nectar 2. (Getränk) fruit drink (*not* pure fruit juice)
	E	nectar:	Nektar - nur G1.

NOTIEREN / **NOTICE**	G notieren:	1. (meist) to make a note of, note (down) 2. (Aktien usw.) to quote / be quoted (*at* a particular price)
	E notice:	zur Kenntnis nehmen, bemerken, merken, wahrnehmen, feststellen

OBJEKT / **OBJECT**	G Objekt:	1. (Grundstück, Haus usw.) property, piece of property 2. (sonst meist) object
	E object:	1. Objekt (*nicht* G1), Gegenstand 2. Ziel

OBJEKTIV / **OBJECTIVE**	G Objektiv:	1. (für Fotoapparat) lens 2. (selten: Foto., Opt.) objective
	E objective:	(meist) Ziel; (comm.) Zielvorstellung; (mil.) Angriffsziel

OBLIGATION / **OBLIGATION**	G Obligation:	(fin.) bond, fixed-interest security
	E obligation:	Verpflichtung

OFFIZIÖS / **OFFICIOUS**	G offiziös (selten):	semi-official
	E officious:	wichtigtuerisch, aufgeblasen, übermäßig dienstbeflissen

N.B. In contrast with its rare German counterpart, E *officious* is quite common, and extremely useful when one needs to be pithily critical of bureaucrats!

ORGAN / **ORGAN**	G Organ:	1. (Biol., Pol. usw.) organ 2. (ugs., Stimme) voice
	E organ:	1. (mus.) Orgel 2. (sonst) Organ - siehe G1.

OTTER / **OTTER**	G Otter, der:	otter
	G Otter, die: (**Kreuzotter**)	adder, (weniger oft) viper
	E otter:	der Otter

167

an **adder** an **otter**

PARKETT / **PARQUET**	G Parkett:	1. (Kino, Theater, Oper) stalls; (AmE) main floor 2. parquet (flooring)
	E parquet:	Parkett - *nur* G2.

PASSAGE / **PASSAGE**	G Passage:	1. (Ladenstraße) (shopping) arcade 2. (sonst) passage
	E passage:	1. Übergang; (Zeit) Verlauf 2. Durchfahrt, Durchreise 3. (See) Schiffsreise, Überfahrt 4. (Buch) Passage 5. (im Gebäude) Gang

PATRONE / **PATRON**	G Patrone:	(für Kugelschreiber, Füllfederhalter) refill, cartridge; (Gewehr) cartridge
	E patron:	1. Kunde, Gast, Besucher (bes. bei Kino, Theater, Gaststätte) 2. Gönner, Mäzen

PETROLEUM / **PETROLEUM**	G Petroleum:	paraffin, (AmE) kerosene
	E petroleum:	Erdöl

PICKEN /	G	**picken:**	1. (herausnehmen, mit Fingern, Gabel usw.) to pick
PICK			2. (Vögel) to peck
	E	**pick:**	1. (meist) (aus)wählen
			2. (Blumen, Früchte usw.) pflücken
POLICE /	G	**Police:**	policy
POLICE	E	**police:**	Polizei
PORZELLAN /	G	**Porzellan:**	1. (hochwertiges Material) porcelain
PORCELAIN			2. (Geschirr im allg., weniger wertvoll) china, crockery
	E	**porcelain:**	Porzellan - *nur* G1.
PRANKE /	G	**Pranke:**	(bei Löwen, Bären usw.) paw
PRANK	E	**prank:**	Streich, Ulk
PREKÄR /	G	**prekär:**	tricky, delicate, embarrassing, awkward; (weniger oft) precarious
PRECARIOUS	E	**precarious:**	gefährlich, unsicher (oft geographisch: *The climber was stuck on a tiny mountain ledge - a very precarious position);* (übertr.) prekär
PRICKELN /	G	**prickeln:**	1. (Haut usw.) to tingle, tickle
PRICKLE			2. (Sekt usw.) to bubble, sparkle
	E	**prickle:**	(Dorn usw.) stechen; (Bart) kratzen; (übertr., z.B. bei Vorfreude) prickeln
PURPUR /	G	**purpur:**	crimson
PURPLE	E	**purple:**	violett, dunkellila
PUZZELN /	G	**puzzeln:**	to do a jigsaw (puzzle)
PUZZLE	E	**puzzle:**	(herum)rätseln

See also **PUZZLE**, p.183.

QUALM / QUALM(S)	G E	Qualm: qualms /kwɑːmz/:	(dense / thick) smoke (meistens im Pl.): Bedenken qualms of conscience = Gewissensbisse

QUARTIER / QUARTER	G	Quartier:	1. (Unterkunft allg.) accommodation 2. (Unterkunft, mil.) quarters
	E	quarter:	1. Viertel (auch Stadtviertel - meist in feststehenden Kombinationen wie *the Latin quarter, the Jewish quarter, the Chinese quarter* usw.) 2. Quartal 3. Pardon: to give no quarter = keinen Pardon geben

QUEUE / QUEUE	G E	Queue: queue:	(billiard) cue (von Leuten) Schlange

RASCH / RASH	G E	rasch: rash:	quick, speedy, rapid, prompt (Handlung) voreilig, überstürzt; (Person) unbesonnen, ungestüm

RATIO / RATIO	G E	Ratio: ratio:	reason, the power / faculty of reason, (Math.) Verhältnis

RATIONELL / RATIONAL	G E	rationell: rational:	efficient, economical vernünftig, rational

REFORMHAUS / REFORM HOUSE	G E	Reformhaus: reform house: (E ist veraltet)	health food shop / store Erziehungsanstalt, Besserungsanstalt

REQUIRIEREN / REQUIRE	G E	requirieren: require:	to requisition, commandeer benötigen, erfordern; (etwas tun) müssen / sollen; verpflichtet sein (etwas zu tun)

REQUISITEN /	G	**Requisiten:**	(Theater) props (= Abkürzung von *properties*)
REQUISITES	E	**requisites:**	Zubehör, Artikel toilet requisites = Toilettenartikel
RESERVATION /	G	**Reservation:**	1. (für Indianer usw.) reservation 2. (veraltet:Sonderrecht) right, discretionary power
RESERVATION	E	**reservation:**	1. (Hotel usw.) Reservierung 2. Vorbehalt, Bedenken 3. siehe G1. N.B. Reservat (Wildpark) = reserve
RESTLOS /	G	**restlos:**	without a trace, complete, total
RESTLESS	E	**restless:**	rastlos, unruhig
RESÜMIEREN /	G	**resümieren:**	to summarize, give a summary of
RESUME	E	**resume:**	wiederaufnehmen
RINGEN /	G	**ringen:**	(Sport) to wrestle; (sonst) to wrestle, to struggle die Hände ringen = to wring one's hands
RING	E	**ring:**	1. anrufen, telefonieren 2. (Türklingel, Telefon) läuten, klingeln
ROLLER /	G	**Roller:**	(Spielzeug) scooter
ROLLER	E	**roller:**	Rolle; Lockenwickler; Walze; Nudelholz; (Meer) Brecher
ROSINE /	G	**Rosine:**	raisin
ROSIN	E	**rosin / resin:**	(Substanz) Harz; (für Violinebogen usw.) Kolophonium
SANIERUNG /	G	**Sanierung:**	1. (Stadtzentrum) redevelopment, renovation, rebuilding 2. (Econ.) revitalisation, making efficient / profitable / viable
SANITATION	E	**sanitation:**	sanitäre Anlagen; Kanalisation; Hygiene

See also **SANIEREN / SANITIZE**, p.121.

| SCHELLFISCH /
SHELLFISH | G Schellfisch:
E shellfish: | haddock
Schalentier(e), Meeresfrüchte |

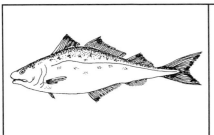
haddock

shellfish

| SEKRET /
SECRET | G Sekret:
E secret: | secretion
Geheimnis |

| SELLERIE /
CELERY | G Sellerie:

E celery: | 1. (Knollen-) celeriac / sə'leriæk /
2. (Stangen-, Stauden-) celery / 'seləri /
siehe *nur* G2. |

celeriac

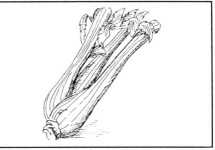
celery

| SPIRALE /
SPIRAL | G Spirale:

E spiral: | 1. (meist, auch übrtr.) spiral
2. (Verhütungsmittel) I.U.D.
(= intrauterine device), (ugs.) coil
(meist) Spirale - aber *nicht* G2.
wage / inflationary spiral =
Lohnspirale / Inflationsspirale
spiral staircase = Wendeltreppe |

| STATIONÄR /
STATIONARY,
STATIONERY | G stationär:
E station*a*ry:
E station*e*ry: | as an in-patient, in hospital
(still)stehend, feststehend, geparkt
Schreibwaren |

STIPENDIUM /	G	**Stipendium:**	scholarship
STIPEND	E	**stipend:**	Gehalt (eines Geistlichen)

STOPPEN /	G	**stoppen:**	1. (meist) to stop
STOP			2. (mit Stoppuhr) to time
	E	**stop:**	aufhören, einstellen, stoppen, verhindern, anhalten usw.

SUBVENTION /	G	**Subvention:**	subsidy, (sehr selten) subvention
SUBVENTION	E	**subvention:**	siehe G Subvention.

SÜFFISANT /	G	**süffisant:**	smug, complacent, self-satisfied
SUFFICIENT	E	**sufficient:**	genug, ausreichend, genügend

TERMINUS /	G	**Terminus:**	(= Terminus technicus): technical term, specialized term
TERMINUS	E	**terminus:**	Endstation

TEXTBUCH /	G	**Textbuch:**	(Mus.) libretto, song-book
TEXTBOOK	E	**textbook:**	Lehrbuch

TRANSPARENT /	G	**Transparent:**	(Spruchband) banner
TRANSPARENT	E	**transparent:**	(nur Adj.) durchsichtig, transparent; (übertr.) eindeutig; durchschaubar

TRANSPIRIEREN /	G	**transpirieren:**	1. (Pflanzen) to transpire
TRANSPIRE			2. (Menschen) to perspire
	E	**transpire:**	passieren, geschehen, bekannt werden, sich ergeben

TRESOR /	G	**Tresor:**	1. (Panzerschrank) safe, strongbox
TREASURE			2. (Raum) strongroom, (bank) vault
	E	**treasure:**	Schatz

TRIBÜNE / TRIBUNE	G	Tribüne:	1. (Fußball usw.) stand Haupttribüne = grandstand 2. (für Redner) platform, rostrum
	E	tribune:	(Volks)tribun

TRICKFILM / TRICK FILM	G	Trickfilm:	1. (Zeichentrickfilm) cartoon (film); animated film 2. (tech.) trick film
	E	trick film:	Trickfilm - *nur* G2.

UNTERARM / UNDERARM	G	Unterarm:	lower arm, forearm
	E	underarm:	1. underarm serve (Sport) = Aufschlag von unten 2. Achselhöhle (aber *armpit* ist viel häufiger)

VASEKTOMIE / VASECTOMY	G	Vasektomie:	1. Gefäßentfernungseingriff 2. (nur Med.) Sterilisationseingriff für Männer
	E	vasectomy:	*nur* G2. N.B. *Vasectomy* ist das normale, gängige Wort für diesen Eingriff - also keine Fachsprache.

WANKEN / WANK	G	wanken:	to sway, shake, wobble, totter
	E	wank (vulg.):	wichsen (= onanieren)

ZIRKEL / CIRCLE	G	Zirkel:	(pair of) compasses /'kʌmpəsɪz/ Magischer Zirkel = Magic Circle
	E	circle:	Kreis

ZYLINDER / CYLINDER	G	Zylinder:	1. (geom.; bei Motoren) cylinder 2. (Hut) top hat, silk hat
	E	cylinder:	1. Zylinder - siehe G1. 2. Flasche (bei Sauerstoffflasche, Gasflasche usw.:) oxygen cylinder, gas cylinder

SECTION L - TEST

Answer the questions, or complete the statements, with a letter in the space on the right.

1. If you had angina, which part of your body would be affected?
   (A) throat   (B) stomach   (C) heart   (D) back   .....

2. If someone humiliates you in public, how do you feel?
   (A) degraded   (B) downgraded   (C) graded   (D) upgraded   .....

3. Where would you go to solve a stationery problem?
   (A) a travel agent   (B) a shop   (C) a station   (D) a hospital   .....

4. Which of these is a synonym for *transpire*?
   (A) perspire   (B) sweat   (C) happen   (D) transpose   .....

5. Which of the following is not a shellfish?
   (A) crab   (B) haddock   (C) lobster   (D) mussel   .....

6. Which of these would not be very useful for a violin bow?
   (A) resin   (B) raisin   (C) rosin   (D) colophony   .....

7. How does an arsonist commit crimes? By ....
   (A) stealing   (B) setting fire to buildings   (C) poisoning   (D) stabbing   .....

8. Catholicism is one type of religious ....
   (A) denomination   (B) profession   (C) confession   (D) procession   .....

9. In which of the following combinations is the word *block* not normally used?
   (A) tower block   (B) mental block   (C) block of ice   (D) writing block   .....

10. What are wine, whisky and beer?
    (A) alcohols   (B) alcoholic drinks   (C) alcoholics   (D) spirits   .....

11. If you are disinterested, it follows that you are ....
    (A) bored   (B) indifferent   (C) uninterested   (D) banned   .....

12. What might be one reasonable way of dealing with a sore throat?
    (A) gargling   (B) giggling   (C) goggling   (D) gurgling   .....

13. If a judge is too kind to a prisoner found guilty, the sentence is too ....
    (A) harsh   (B) lenient   (C) mild   (D) softly   .....

14. A synonym for *to write something down* is to .... something.
    (A) remark   (B) make a note of   (C) notice   (D) mention   .....

15. Which of these colours is a sort of *red*, rather than a mixture of red and blue?
    (A) lilac   (B) violet   (C) purple   (D) crimson   .....

16. Which of the following is a kind of device?
    (A) a 10-dollar note   (B) a Eurocheque   (C) a mixer   (D) a loan in Yen   .....

17. Which of these does not exist in any normal football competition?
    (A) final   (B) finale   (C) semi-final   (D) quarter-final   .....

18. What sort of people can go for regular walks in cloisters?
    (A) monks   (B) nuns   (C) Oxbridge students   (D) all of the last three   .....

19. Who would be particularly interested in libel suits?
    (A) botanists   (B) tailors   (C) lawyers   (D) biologists   .....

20. An objective normally refers to a ....
    (A) goal   (B) piece of property   (C) camera lens   (D) telescope   .....

21. If you had *no qualms* about something, you would not be troubled by ....
    (A) hesitation   (B) your conscience   (C) smoke   (D) small insects

22. What are the articles used in a theatre to make a play more realistic?
    (A) requisites   (B) requirements   (C) requisitions   (D) props   .....

23. Which of these cannot be a synonym for the other three?
    (A) without a trace   (B) restlessly   (C) completely   (D) totally   .....

24. If you wanted to resume something, you would .... it.
    (A) carry on with   (B) write a resumé of   (C) summarize   (D) presume   .....

25. If you broke your axle, where would you go?
    (A) garage   (B) church   (C) hospital   (D) prison   .....

26. Which of the following does not exist?
    (A) sponge   (B) sponge biscuit   (C) sponge cake   (D) sponge finger   .....

27. Which of the following would normally be found at sea?
    (A) hard hat   (B) helmet   (C) safety helmet   (D) helm   .....

28. Which of the following offers gratification as an essential part of his job?
    (A) bank manager   (B) gigolo   (C) priest   (D) factory manager   .....

29. Where are you most likely to find a commode?
    (A) old people's home   (B) kindergarten   (C) furniture shop   (D) school   .....

30. Which of these cannot be fired from a weapon?
    (A) cartridge   (B) shell   (C) patron   (D) bullet   .....

31. To cover yourself against fire damage, you take out an insurance ....
    (A) policy   (B) politic   (C) police   (D) any of the last three   .....

32. Which of these cannot be a synonym for the other three?
    (A) reason   (B) argument   (C) quarrel   (D) row   .....

33. Which of these would not normally serve meals to non-residents?
    (A) pub   (B) guest-house   (C) inn   (D) restaurant   .....

34. Which of these cannot be a synonym for invalidity?
    (A) disability (B) worthlessness (C) non-qualification (D) handicap

35. Which of these can grow on the sides of a man's face?
    (A) sideburns (B) cutlets (C) chops (D) buttercups

36. Which of these cannot have wings?
    (A) grouse (B) kite (C) shrimp (D) dragonfly

37. Which of these is a type of snake?
    (A) adder (B) prank (C) slug (D) otter

38. From which of these could you not normally watch a football match?
    (A) stand (B) terraces (C) tribunes (D) grandstand

39. Which of these does not normally live in the sea?
    (A) herring (B) prawn (C) crab (D) muscle

40. Which of the following cannot be a part of the body?
    (A) nag (B) nape (C) neck (D) tonsil

41. What would you do with a bread crumb to remove it from a tablecloth?
    (A) flatter it (B) flutter it (C) flick it (D) flatten it

42. Which of the following is an accurate description of Mozart?
    (A) genial (B) a genius (C) a genie (D) a gene

43. What do flags do in a light wind? They ....
    (A) hoist (B) flatten (C) flatter (D) flutter

44. Which word describes a childish trick or joke?
    (A) prank (B) paw (C) cue (D) coil

45. What is the word for financial support given to a gifted university student?
    (A) subvention (B) stipend (C) scholarship (D) subsidy

46. Which of these has no medical connotation?
    (A) an I.U.D. (B) vasectomy (C) a spiral (D) an organ

47. Which of these cannot be a meaning of *reservation* ?
    (A) booking (B) worry (C) home for Indians (D) wildlife park

48. Which of these is not a synonym for the other three?
    (A) speedy (B) prompt (C) rash (D) rapid

49. Which of the following is not edible?
    (A) a kipper (B) a lime (C) a melon (D) a J.C.B.

50. What is the verb to describe what champagne does in a glass?
    (A) tingle (B) prickle (C) sparkle (D) tickle

SECTION M – PSEUDO-ANGLICISMS

Pseudo-anglicisms are English (or English-looking) words or phrases which cannot be used in English as they are used in German. They fall broadly into three categories:

(1) Words which exist in English, but with a **different meaning** either all or some of the time. In type, they are therefore similar in many respects to the false friends which make up the bulk of this volume. Examples are: *Box, clever, Flipper, Gag, Gully, pink, Pudding, Sets, Spleen.*
Entries in this category are not marked with an asterisk.

(2) Words which have a slightly **different form** in English, but whose meaning is the same, or nearly the same. Examples are: *Aircondition, Facelifting, Happy-End, last not least, open-end.*
Entries in this category are marked with a single asterisk: *

(3) Words which are **non-existent** in English. Examples are: *Barkeeper, Dressman, Hometrainer, No-Name, Pullunder, Radiorecorder, Talkmaster, Twen.*
Entries in this category are marked with a double asterisk: **

Quite a number fall into both categories (1) and (2), especially verbs. *Catchen*, for example, exhibits both a germanicised form and a different meaning from English, as do *jobben, kicken, steppen* and *trampen*.

As you might expect, there are a handful that defy categorisation: hybrids like *Chesterkäse* ; dated expressions like *Freak* ; and puzzling oddities like *Merry Old England*. In the main, however, the threefold categorisation holds good.

The following collection lays no claim to completeness; that would be impossible. The actual number of pseudo-anglicisms is clearly large and constantly growing, and the best we can hope to do is spotlight some of the commonest and most useful for German speakers to be aware of. Remember that (Sw.) refers to Swiss German usage.

Pseudo-anglicism	*Real English*	*Comment*
Aircondition *	airconditioning	
Airfresh *	air freshener	
Allround-man *	all-rounder	
(Auto)skooter	dodgem	*scooter* = Roller (See also **ROLLER / ROLLER**, p.170.
Autostop	hitch-hiking	

Barkeeper **	barman / barmaid (AmE) bartender	
Beefsteak, deutsches	meatball, rissole, faggot	E *beefsteak* can only mean *steak:* a slice of beef, not made from mince.
Blackout	mental block	*Blackout* - in *'to have a blackout'* - is real English if you are talking about s.o. losing consciousness.
Boiler (Durchlauferhitzer)	water-heater	In most other senses, e.g. boiler for a central heating system, boiler in a factory or on a ship, E *boiler* and G *Boiler* are true friends.
Box (für Stereo)	(loud)speaker	Note also: die Boxen = *the pits* (in motor-racing).
Brain-Trust *	panel of experts	E *brains trust* exists, with a similar meaning to the German, but is very rare nowadays.
Callboy	male prostitute (getting clients by phone)	But note that German *Callgirl* = English *call-girl*. *Callboy* exists as a theatrical word: it is the name for the person who tells actors when they have to go on stage.
Camping-Platz*	camp-site	*Camping* is the name of the hobby, not the name of a place to practise it.
Caravan	estate car, (AmE) station wagon	*Caravan* in English means only *Wohnwagen*.
catchen *	to do catch / all-in wrestling	
Catcher	catch / all-in wrestler	
checken * (ugs.)	to understand	When used to mean *kontrollieren,* (e.g. med., tech.) checken = *to check*
Chesterkäse **	nil	*Chester*, the county town of Cheshire, exists; *Cheshire cheese* exists; but German *Chesterkäse* is more like English cheddar cheese than Cheshire cheese.
Chips	crisps, (AmE) chips	*Chips* in Britain means *french fries*, i.e. the same as *Pommes frites*.

City	town centre, (AmE) downtown	Beware! Most foreign learners overuse the word *city*. It is usually reserved for very big places - say 100,000 people or more.
Clan	clique	*Clan* is reserved for talk of Scottish family lines.
Clinch (übertr.)	nil	*Clinch* is only used to describe two boxers (or lovers!) locked together. Figuratively, in the meaning of a verbal dispute, you need a rewrite: *Die waren im Clinch* = They were going at each other / They were getting stuck into each other / They were at loggerheads.
Container	skip (for rubbish), bottle bank (for bottles)	E *container* normally means *Behälter,* and covers all shapes and sizes from a gas-holder to a tiny pill-box. It is also used (as in German) for the objects carried by *container ships*.
Crack (= Expert)	ace, expert	The word is still used in English only in the expression *'he's a crack shot'*, meaning *he's an expert with the gun*. With reference to drugs, G *Crack* = E *crack*.
Dancing	dance-hall	Mainly Austrian usage. cf. Camping-Platz, p.178.
Dealer (Rauschgift)	pusher	*Dealer* can be used with the same meaning, but is less common.
Derby (Sw.)	ordeal	E derby / ˈdɑːbi/ is useful mainly in the phrase *the local derby*, used in sport to denote a match between two rival clubs in the same area, e.g. a football match between Manchester United and Manchester City. *The Derby* is the name of a famous annual horse race held in Epsom, Surrey, since 1780.
Dreß	(sports) kit / gear, outfit, (esp. football) strip	*Dress* means *Kleid* ; in phrases like *formal dress* or *casual dress*, it means *Kleidung*.
Dressman **	male model	

Drops *	fruit drop	
Evergreen	(for songs:) old favourite, golden oldie, standard (n.);	E *evergreen* = immergrüne(r) Baum / Pflanze.
Facelifting *	face-lift	See also **Lift / liften**.
Flipper	pinball machine	English *flipper* = Flosse - both for animals and sub-aqua enthusiasts.
Flirt	flirtation	In English, a *flirt* can only refer to a *person* who behaves in a flirtatious way.
Folklore	folk music, folk singing, folk dancing - or some combination of the three.	*Folklore* refers in English almost exclusively to the telling, or handing down, of fairy-tales, (local) legends, etc.
fooden * (Sw.)	to eat	
Freak	fan, enthusiast, buff	This is mainly a frequency point: *freak* was used extensively to mean *enthusiast / buff*, especially in the sixties, but is rarely heard nowadays.
Gag (= Besonderheit)	gimmick, stunt, (humorous) special effect	*Gag* in English normally refers to a joke told on stage by a stand-up comedian.
Gangsterboß *	gang boss, gang leader	
Goalgetter **	(goal-)scorer	
Grill	(usually) barbecue - for cooking over charcoal out of doors	*Grill* is the part of a normal English cooker under which you make toast; *grille* refers to a car radiator front.
Gully	drain (in the gutter)	English *gully* = Schlucht, Rinne
Ham and eggs	bacon and eggs	*Ham* is boiled or smoked; *bacon* is fried or grilled. The British don't eat ham for breakfast.
Happy-End *	happy end*ing*	

Hitliste	hit parade, "the charts"	A *hit list* in English refers to a list of people that some radical group, e.g. of terrorists, wishes to kill.
Hometrainer **	exercise bike; (less often) rowing-machine, step-machine, etc.	The English translation obviously depends on the type of *fitness machine* referred to. cf. **Trainer**, p.184.
Hosteß (auf Reisen)	courier, rep. (= representative)	In the other two meanings (lady on aeroplane; euphemism for prostitute), *hostess* is also used in English.
Insider-Tip **	tip	
jobben *	to work, to do temporary work	*Job* is only a noun in English.
Jury	panel, panel of judges	*Jury* means *die Geschworenen* in a law court. It also occasionally gets used in the German sense for TV shows, e.g. Juke-box Jury.
kicken * (für eine Mannschaft)	to play (football)	Kicker = football / soccer player
last not least *	last *but* not least	
Lift / liften (ugs.)	face-lift / to give s.o. a face-lift	*To give s.o. a lift* in Britain is used only in the context of a *Mitfahrgelegenheit*, which is why you can't abbreviate *face-lift*. *Lift (AmE: elevator) also* = Fahrstuhl. See also **Facelifting.**
Looping	looping the loop	*Einen Looping machen* = to loop the loop
Make-up (= flüssige Creme)	foundation cream	In the *general* cosmetic sense, E *Make-up* = G Make-up. *Make-up (in theatre)* = die Maske
Manchester (veraltet)	thick / heavy / jumbo cord	Both in English and German these words are becoming as dated as the material they refer to, but *cord jeans, cord trousers* and *cords* are still in common use.
Merry Old England	nil	Where German speakers got this from, and why it is so popular, is a bit of a mystery. It is not used.

Minigolf	crazy golf	Another frequency point: *mini-golf* is very occasionally found with the same meaning as in German, but is far from usual.
Musikbox	juke-box	E *music box* = Spieluhr
No-Name(-Produkt) **	(unbranded goods) More often: a rewrite, e.g. "What sort of computer have you got?" "Oh, it's **not a famous make**."	Not only the word but also the phenomenon of selling unbranded goods is almost completely unknown in Britain. Famous producers often supply large retail chains with goods which are then sold on as **own brand** goods, with the *chain's name* on them.
Oldtimer	(pre-1917:) **veteran car**, (AmE) antique car; (1917 - 1930:) **vintage car**, (AmE) classic car	*Oldtimer* is a rare word in English, but when it is used, it usually refers - affectionately - to people, or sometimes animals, but not cars. Pre-1905 cars are called **true veterans** (AmE: true antiques).
open-end * (adj.)	open-*ended*	
Pamphlet	lampoon, satirical leaflet/brochure etc.	English *pamphlet* (= Broschüre, Flugblatt) is completely neutral in tone.
pink	shocking pink	English *pink* = rosa.
Playback (beim Singen)	miming; rewrite with *to mime*	E *playback* = Wiedergabe (on tape recorders etc.)
Pony, der	fringe, (AmE) bangs	E *pony* = **das** Pony.
Pudding	blancmange, vanilla / chocolate pudding	English **Pudding** = *Nachtisch, Dessert*. The English word is much broader in reference than the German but it often crops up in specific dessert names like *summer pudding, Christmas pudding, bread-and-butter pudding*.
Pullunder **	sleeveless pullover	
Punchingball *	punch-ball	

Punker *	punk	Note that E *punk* is both a noun (for a person) and an adjective, as in *punk music*.
Puzzle	jigsaw puzzle, jigsaw	See also **PUZZELN / PUZZLE**, p.168.
Radiorecorder *	cassette radio, radio cassette, radio / cassette recorder	The third option given, 'radio / cassette recorder', is always used with *all three words* mentioned, i.e. it is never shortened.
Roastbeef	(if raw:) sirloin of beef; (if roast:) (roast) beef sirloin	E *roast beef* = Rinderbraten
Rowdy	lout, hooligan, yob, vandal; (much less often) rowdy	Note that (1) *rowdy* in English is usually an adjective; (2) its meaning is milder than the German. *Rowdy* neighbours would mean *noisy* neighbours - but not vandals. Note also **Straßenrowdy / Verkehrsrowdy** = *road hog*.
Sets (auf dem Tisch)	place mats, tablemats	
Shakehands *	handshake	
Shower (Sw.)	show-off	
Showmaster **	host, compère; (less often) M.C. (= Master of Ceremonies)	
Skooter	See (**Auto)skooter**, p.177.	
Slip	(under)pants, briefs, (ladies') knickers, (AmE) panties	*Slip* has a vast number of meanings in English: *Unterrock* and *Flüchtigkeitsfehler* are probably the commonest.
Slipper	slip-on shoe, (AmE) loafer	English *slippers* = Hausschuhe.
Smoking	dinner-jacket, (AmE) tuxedo	E *smoking* = das Rauchen
Sonnyboy	"Prince Charming"	E *sonny boy* (oder *sonny Jim*) = mein Junge (form of verbal address)

Spleen	crazy notion / idea, peculiar / eccentric habit, eccentricity	E *spleen* = Milz *to vent one's spleen on s.o.* = seine Wut (an jdm.) auslassen
Spot	commercial, ad.	
steppen *	(Tanz) to tap-dance; (Tagesdecken usw.) to quilt	E *to step* = treten - and many other meanings.
surfen *	to **wind**surf / board-sail	**Surfing** (Wellenreiten) and **windsurfing** are two distinct sports; if you try to abbreviate *windsurfing* in an English-speaking country, you will always be misunderstood.

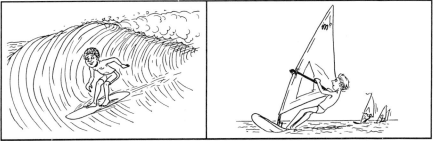

surfing   windsurfing / (less often) **boardsailing**

Talkmaster **	(chat-show) host; (AmE) (talk-show) host	
Teens	teenagers	*Teens* in English refers not directly to young people, but their age. Thus *"Tim will be in his teens next year"* means he's 12 now.
Trainer (Sw., = (Trainingsanzug)	tracksuit	A *trainer* in English is usually a person (esp. in sport), sometimes a shoe (esp. running shoe), and very occasionally a machine (e.g. for training air pilots). cf. **Hometrainer**, p.181.
trampen *	to hitchhike, go hitchhiking	*to tramp* = stapfen, stampfen, marschieren; *to tramp around* = herumstiefeln
Twen **	s.o. in his / her twenties	
Whirlpool	jacuzzi / dʒə'kuːzi /	E *Whirlpool* = Strudel

FINAL TEST

Each of the following contains one false friend or pseudo-anglicism. Underline it in pencil, then replace it on the right with a correct word or phrase.

CORRECTION

1. The officer has commandeered whole palettes of tinned food, and consequently his unit disposes of a good store of food.

2. Several of my fellow pupils, who were good mimics, could imitate our housemaster's absurdly refined accent, with which he tried to appear mundane.

3. He was discussing pay and conditions across Europe and cited the instance of the general lack of Christmas gratifications paid to civil servants in Britain.

4. Clive was a notorious exhibitionist, who would often take his friends out to feudal restaurants and embarrass them by treating them to extravagant meals.

5. We students were very much amused to read in a scurrilous exposé in the Sunday Smut that our tutor was a spanner well known to the Oxford police.

6. She grinned as she mixed the arson into the pudding that she was going to serve to her beast of a husband, who had been unfaithful to her for years.

7. He's a crack flipper player who displays exemplary expertise in his technique: you'll never beat him.

8. Some very lifelike dragons contributed to the spectacle of the carnival and met with an enthusiastic resonance from the crowd.

9. According to reliable sources, our pompous and respectable Lord Mayor was seen last night in the company of some well-known callboys and so-called hostesses.

10. Our party's manifest clearly states that we shall set up a commission to consider ways of ensuring that important tariffs are further reduced.

11. The crux of the matter is to establish how we can restrict the availability of alcoholics to people in their teens without imposing an actual ban.

	CORRECTION

12. It is not social to lower the tax on frivolous luxuries like pearl necklaces and to raise it on foods like fish and chips.

13. No, I haven't made a testament, although my solicitor keeps nagging me to - no doubt so that he can charge a hefty fee.

14. He managed to resume all his arguments against the new libel law in a single paragraph.

15. There's nothing wrong with the playback on this tape deck or with the boxes on your stereo: it's just that you've inserted a blank tape by mistake!

16. This guest-house must range among the worst I've ever stayed in: I think that kipper I had for breakfast was as antique as the central heating system.

17. He owns what must be the definitive collection of 18th-century porcelain, but it's a pity he has to keep it in a treasure all the time.

18. He went to Milan to exercise his Italian, but unintentionally said something very offensive to a policeman, and ended up in jail.

19. It was a fatal mistake to go to Dr. Fumble: it's vital that you find a proper doctor who can heal that gastritis of yours.

20. We've got most of the requisites for the play: we just need one more thing, namely a music box of the sort you'd see in an 18th-century drawing-room.

21. This rocket will carry the new space probe into orbit: it should be a success, as international capacities have collaborated in its design.

22. I can't see the object of playing the national hymn at the end of the film, when most patrons are in a hurry to get out of the cinema and get a drink in the nearest pub.

23. The size of the premium is obviously an important moment when you are deciding which insurance policy to choose, but it is rash automatically to select the cheapest one.

24. These melons are grown by monks in a local cloister, and they have a beautiful delicate colour as well as a delicious taste.

CORRECTION

25. This picture of a huntsman with his dog and his flint is by an artist best known for his grandiose landscapes.

26. His bigoted views make him intolerant of the ideas and concepts of any confession except his own.

27. Every member of a jury should be a completely disinterested party, but no doubt it is blue-eyed to believe this is always the case in real life.

28. It would be accurate to say she is obsessed with hygiene, and you won't find a corn of dust on her parquet floor.

29. She unashamedly admitted that she had overslept, rather than swindling to explain why she had not been punctual.

30. She demonstratively ignored the rules of protocol and remained seated when the Prince entered the room, behaviour which His Highness graciously overlooked.

31. The Philosophy Seminar is full of academics who have a patent lack of intelligence, despite their supreme arrogance.

32. I know he lives near a railway terminus, but is that a good motive for giving him the British Rail coursebook for his birthday?

33. It is not very human to hunt foxes or otters or hares - in fact I think such so-called sport degrades the people who practise it.

34. The potency of the wine was such that even your virtuous sister began to behave in a less than solid manner.

35. If this government had managed to pursue a competent economic policy, there would be less economic misery and perhaps also less criminality in this country of ours.

36. I won't marry him even if he is one of the local prominence: a man who's not a bit clever and walks like a crab has no allure for me.

37. You may say this is a noble race of dog, but it is still remarkably stupid and it also gives off a very pungent smell.

38. Unfortunately we live in a very loud street: several of our neighbours have no qualms about playing heavy metal music at full volume at two in the morning.

CORRECTION

39. I know the principles of bridge construction: I absolved a course in civil engineering some years ago and I've still got all the textbooks.

40. There was an animated discussion on the subject of herring quotas: outside the Houses of Parliament fishermen carrying transparents demonstrated against the provisions of the new EC law.

41. The music was so loud that after trying to get to sleep I resigned and read a book, though I couldn't concentrate on it as a large meal of shellfish had left me feeling restless and even slightly ill.

42. I was flattered by the invitation to coffee and biscuits in the officers' mess, but the conversation there was so technical that I was soon swimming.

43. These angina attacks have become so serious that you need stationary treatment, though of course there's no real cure for the condition.

44. Most film actors would use a double for a stunt like that, and I assume he just doesn't realise how dangerous it is.

45. Gurgling with hot lemon is hardly sufficient treatment for this tropical fever: you require proper medical treatment.

46. The feeling in the party basis is that we are a sovereign state that should quit this sort of international body rather than make further concessions to unreasonable demands.

47. It's a hopeless shop: they didn't have stationery of the format I required or even a new mine for my ballpoint.

48. I don't think we have a Polish-Swedish lexicon, but I can check in the store if you don't mind waiting a moment.

49. That consignment of slippers James Footwear promised for yesterday still hasn't arrived: you'd better ring their expedition and complain.

50. I've bought this enormous book on first aid, but I can't even find out how to put on a bandage because there isn't a decent register.

51. She ruined her figure by eating ten bars of nougat every day, which she put down to the boredom of doing repetitive accord work.

CORRECTION

52. It transpired that she hadn't got the flu at all but was merely simulating so that she could stay at home and watch the tennis final on TV.

53. Ever since he was made head of the environmental resort he thinks he holds far too exalted a position to be seen stapling the pages of some pamphlets together.

54. We will continue to have personal shortages unless we increase the appeal of our firm to prospective applicants by undertaking a thorough revision of the pay structure.

55. A new boiler can be very expensive, but I happen to know someone in the branch, and he can also get you the ventilator you need to draw off the fumes.

56. These moors may look barren and forbidding, but they represent our existence to us hill farmers, and it would cause us real mental agony to have to leave them.

57. An inspection of the tachometer revealed it was giving a completely wrong indication of the car's speed.

58. The real trouble is that my wife finds the spiral doesn't suit her, and she thinks I ought to have a vasectomy.

59. She's a terrible flirt: she was at that fete that Peter and Ann had at their new house and I heard her telling that awful Steve what a brilliant genius he is.

60. I know it's a chore taking things back to a shop and reclaiming, but consumers must exercise their rights and, besides, it gives you the chance to vent your spleen.

61. I was puzzled by the ease with which I got an attest from Dr. Spume: I didn't even have to take my vest off, let alone undergo a thorough examination.

62. Just because some ageing sonny boy stands her veal cutlets and takes her to a casino, she thinks she belongs to some exclusive clique of jet-setters.

63. "Right," said the animator, "I want you all to clap together when the Prince comes on stage and hiss and boo when the Wicked Witch appears."

64. The ancient choir has a distinct flair of medieval mystery: it is indeed a tribute to the enormously skilful workmanship of the unknown wood-carver.

65. Our mode correspondent has had a sneak preview of the new bathing costumes and reports that she felt a mild shock when she saw how revealing they are.

66. It's a tick of his to wear a purple waistcoat whenever he eats out, even if he just has cheese and pickle sandwiches at his local.

67. I know that the TV spot shows the car going round a chicane at breakneck speed, but it's more important to know how many miles to the gallon the vehicle does.

68. Our son has got two weeks house arrest for hiding a banana skin in Uncle Joe's slippers and pouring condensed milk into my radio cassette - hardly harmless pranks!

69. The central government's decision to reduce the frequency of the train service on this line met with a chorus of protest from all the communes affected.

70. The vicar incurred great censure from Mr. Justice Purselip for showing Disney trick films in the chapel and thereby, as he claimed, defiling it.

71. As he flicked through the pages of his well-worn address book, the depraved Sir Jasper Tentacle felt his skin prickle with anticipation at the thought of sharing his whirlpool with one of his many girlfriends.

72. That big businessman is no longer liquid, and all the chicanery of his smart lawyers may postpone his bankruptcy, but it won't prevent it.

73. Canon Symes was seized with jealousy when his householder, who had been with him for twenty years, eventually married the Reverend Sponge.

74. Picking the right cutlery and sets, and thereby creating an elegant atmosphere, are indirectly a part of the art of gastronomy, I suppose, but such things are hardly as vital as being able to cook roast beef to perfection.

75. That head-on collision on the tangent looked worse than it actually was: one motorist strained his neck muscles quite badly and needed a few stitches, but the other one was completely unhurt.

CORRECTION

CORRECTION

76. I don't think that this silly plaster plastic of our managing director is a suitable way of honouring him for his contribution to the company while he was still at the helm.

77. There's some concern that the fusion of these two construction companies will hinder genuine competition in the industry.

78. The Government has a mandate to sanitize the steel industry, but not to demolish it completely, which is what will happen if this scheme is adopted.

79. Look at the way he's commanding those poor decorators about! Anyone would think he had never retired from the marines!

80. The general economic constellation suggests that the rational policy would be to encourage an increase in the ratio of manufacturing to service jobs.

KEY TO EXERCISES

Section A

A. 1. done / taken
    2. horror / wretch
    3. neat and tidy
    4. grass roots / rank and file
    5. generator
    6. encouraged / prompted / stimulated
    7. spellbound
    8. bigoted / intolerant
    9. Those involved / The participants
    10. sick-note / medical certificate
    11. bandage
    12. blanks / gaps

B. 1. He's doing piecework /
        He's on piecework.
    2. antique furniture
    3. Egyptian antiquities
    4. sheer / utter / complete nonsense
    5. a blank (cartridge)
    6. neat handwriting (N.B. no 'a'!)
    7. of one's own accord
    8. brake-unit

C. (a) antic
    (b) blank
    (c) basis
    (d) antiquity
    (e) aggregate
    (f) animator
    (g) antique
    (h) to ban s.o.
    (i) base

    (8) an absurd action or childish trick
    (5) a harmless cartridge or bullet fired from a gun
    (2) the starting-point, or fundamentals, for a discussion
    (10) the far distant past
    (9) the sum total
    (12) s.o. who creates the illusion of movement (in a film)
    (3) an old object, often collected for its beauty or value
    (15) to forbid or exclude s.o. from entering a place
    (6) s.th. to rest a statue or ornament on

D. 1. T
    2. F are often kept in / not allowed out
    3. T
    4. T
    5. F s.o. who is narrow-minded and intolerant
    6. T

Section B

A.
1. CHORE	goes with	BORING ROUTINE TASK
2. DISPOSE OF	goes with	GET RID OF
3. FIELD	goes with	LINE OF BUSINESS
4. DEMOLISH	goes with	PULL DOWN
5. BLEND	goes with	MIXTURE
6. AT A LOW EBB	goes with	DEPRESSED
7. CHORUS	goes with	REFRAIN
8. DECORATOR	goes with	PAINTER
9. APERTURE	goes with	F-NUMBER
10. DELICATE	goes with	SENSITIVE

B. 1. with the gloves off / with no holds barred
    2. causeway
    3. problem / trouble
    4. a(n) absolute / complete beginner
    5. stand-in
    6. pointedly
    7. crowd
    8. graduates
    9. certified

C. 1. dragon   2. kite   3. dragons   4. hang-glider   5. hang-glider

D. 1. set   2. décor   3. window dressing   4. decoration

E. 1. a strong blend of tea / tea mixture
    2. He absolved him from his sins.
    3. The tide is going out - soon the sea will be 500 metres away.
    4. classical architecture
    5. He's not his usual self / not in good shape / not fit today.
    6. the crux / heart / core of the problem
    7. She gave us a definite no.
    8. The floor was shining / shiny.

Section C

A. 1. dispatch
    2. fête
    3. physique
    4. posh
    5. numbers
    6. class
    7. embarrassing
    8. atmosphere
    9. dirty
    10. fatal
    11. detailed
    12. exposé
    13. flasher
    14. full-frontal
    15. livelihood

B. 1. T
    2. F   many **drafts / outlines**
    3. F   you **stamp** your letters
    4. T
    5. T
    6. F   are often **drilled**
    7. T
    8. F   to **certify**

C. 1. You've got the job? That's great / terrific / fantastic!, etc.
    2. hay fever
    3. glandular fever
    4. to take s.o.'s temperature
    5. I'm deadly serious.
    6. the dyke at Wilhelmshaven
    7. the participants / those involved in the hijack
    8. This bitch has stolen my husband.
    9. Don't look for a job in the coal industry: the whole industry is going downhill.
    10. a very neat and tidy flat
    11. a delicate / tricky problem
    12. a household chore

Section D

A. 1. Gulf - Bay
    2. graceful
    3. humane
    4. for a service / to be serviced
    5. pay (a fee to)
    6. peddling
    7. anniversary
    8. hinder
    9. grand / splendid, etc.
    10. caretaker

B. 1. F   It can!
    2. F   *Intelligence* is mental capacity; *the intelligentsia* are intelligent people
    3. F   you advertise it
    4. T
    5. F   Farmers hoe
    6. T
    7. T

C. (a) indication   *(10) a sign*
    (b) jubilee   *(12) anniversary of monarch's reign or lengthy marriage*
    (c) grandiose   *(11) pretentious, ostentatious or overdone*
    (d) to house   *(8) to accommodate*
    (e) graceful   *(17) elegant*
    (f) fatal   *(9) death-bringing*
    (g) grand   *(15) gracious or highly cultivated*
    (h) crux   *(16) essential point; the heart of the matter*
    (i) to peddle   *(1) to hawk*
    (j) hefty   *(7) heavy*

D. 1. a nice crowd / bunch
    2. to do piece-work
    3. What authority / department can I apply to?
    4. They only employ graduates.
    5. subsistence level
    6. She puts on airs and graces.
    7. We don't yet know that for sure / We don't know that definitely yet.
    8. This town has got a certain atmosphere.

E. 1. Yes - as long as they have a franking machine.
    2. Yes
    3. Yes
    4. No - Decorators paint; window dressers dress windows.
    5. No - Flashers are arrested if seen by the police.
    6. Yes
    7. Yes
    8. No - they write detailed reports.

Section E

A. 1. an expert / an authority
    2. certify
    3. boss people about / around
    4. responsible
    5. vandalized / smashed up
    6. draft
    7. head-on collision
    8. crux / heart / core
    9. local authority / town council
    10. clear

11. figure
12. designer / design engineer
13. caricature
14. drilling
15. posh / fancy
16. cure
17. putty
18. courts
19. examination board / board of examiners
20. Fold up

B.
1. confectionery - *(r) sweets*
2. canon - *(l) a kind of priest*
3. concerto - *(n) a musical composition for orchestra and 1 or 2 soloists*
4. commission - *(m) money earned as an agent for selling goods or services*
5. cannon - *(q) one or more guns which can fire heavy metal balls*
6. kernel - *(p) the edible part of a nut, inside the shell*
7. concentrated - *(s) made more dense, intense or pure*
8. concept - *(c) an idea or notion*
9. commune - *(j) a living unit, e.g. five people in one house*
10. to commandeer - *(a) to requisition*

C.
1. six point seven
2. nought point four   (AmE: zero point four)
3. You buy evaporated milk in tins   (AmE: in cans)
4. The courts can't help you.
5. The meal was really awful / lousy / (esp. AmE:) the pits, etc.
6. Who is responsible for such matters?
7. Cherry stones are bigger than grape pips.
8. mincemeat / minced meat / mince
9. You've got a double!
10. stage fright
11. His clothing / The way he dresses is flamboyant.
12. He was punished as an example (to others)`.

Section F

A.
1. T
2. F trade fair
3. F ..number of seats
4. T
5. T
6. F new refills
7. F 25-volume encyclopaedia
8. T
9. T
10. F tins / (AmE) cans
11. T
12. T
13. F country(side)
14. T
15. F crime is increasing
16. F at the second hearing / on appeal
17. F prevented from
18. F G**u**lf
19. F 'Excursion' = trip 'Field trip' = scientific / research trip
20. T

B.   1. country   2. countryside   3. countryside   4. land   5. land

C.   1. mass   2. mess   3. fair   4. mess   5. fair

D.   1. plan   2. concept   3. draft

E. 1. (facial) expressions   6. crisis   11. caretaker
    2. costumes   7. factor   12. concertos
    3. fix / see to   8. noisy   13. Intelligence
    4. pretends   9. antiques   14. bilingual secretary
    5. treatment (there is   10. budget
       no cure)

Section G

A. 1. moor(s)   2. bogs   3. fens   4. bog

B. 1. game   2. catch   3. part   4. there / involved

C. 1. Yes   7. Yes
    2. No - a personal manager   8. No - a novella
    3. Yes   9. No - posh / fancy
    4. No - pushy / insistent   10. Yes
    5. Yes   11. No - glass beads
    6. No - hard and white   12. No - a sophisticated / elegant life

D. 1. lots of tenants   9. pushy   17. confectionery
    2. tenants   10. nougat   18. mundane
    3. flamboyant   11. patent   19. kit
    4. posh   12. because   20. grins
    5. notorious   13. section   21. authority
    6. offensive   14. landscapes   22. concept
    7. novel   15. palette   23. pretend
    8. pearls   16. Personnel

Section H

A. 1. given me a receipt   6. rehearsal   11. quota
    2. policy   7. spots / pimples   12. clever / cunning
    3. sculpture   (AmE:) zits   13. potency
    4. secular   8. bonus   14. tarpaulin
    5. V.I.P.s /   9. random   15. ostentatious / grandiose
       top people   10. minutes

B. 1. F - great / wonderful, etc.   6. T
    2. F - can prompt / stimulate   7. T
    3. F - ..haven't made other   8. F - ...employ window dressers
       plans / arrangements   9. T
    4. F - ..is called a field trip   10. T
    5. T   11. F - A cartoon is ...

C. 1. a local   (q) a pub close to your home
   2. a conserve   (c) an unusual word for high-quality jam
   3. a medallion   (j) a large medal, often used for show or decoration
   4. a mine   (l) a place to extract coal, copper, tin, etc.
   5. misery   (k) extreme unhappiness and / or extreme poverty
   6. a carnival   (u) a colourful summer event used to raise money for charity
   7. a cure   (o) s.th.that is capable of getting rid of a disease
   8. to insert   (f) to put into
   9. a mandate   (h) official public support for a government or a policy
   10. a mimic   (a) a person who is good at copying others' mannerisms

D. 1. one point five
   2. I can't concentrate on my work today.
   3. He has been released on parole.
   4. The children are getting too noisy.
   5. to be away on a job
   6. Hans wants to become a designer / design engineer.
   7. Did it work out all right with the journey?
   8. a grain of sand
   9. The crime rate is rising.
   10. The receptionist always wears a smart (two-piece) suit.
   11. I've bought you a box of chocolates.
   12. I hope you can benefit from this course.

Section I

A. 1. missiles   11. repay your hospitality / reciprocate
   2. is giving a paper   12. response
   3. realise   13. column
   4. complain about   14. department
   5. bloody-mindedness   15. pattern / layout
   6. made profitable   16. index
   7. is at a loss / is lost   17. neat and tidy
   8. ranks   18. dummies
   9. fair / decent / reasonable 19. predicate
   10. breed   20. revision

B. 1. peel   4. shell   7. shell   10. skin
   2. rind   5. skin   8. rind   11. shell
   3. bark   6. crust   9. skin   12. skin

C. 1. No - illogical / inconsistent   6. Yes
   2. Yes   7. No - it's pejorative
   3. No - an encyclopaedia   8. Yes - e.g. if he's yawning loudly
      or dictionary   9. Yes
   4. Yes   10. No - it's a common medical instrument
   5. Yes

D.
1. foreign policy
2. beads of sweat
3. a random sample
4. to give prominence to s.th.
5. random breath tests
6. I'll pull the strings / show them who's boss / paint the town red
7. prim and proper
8. elegant / stylish / sophisticated clothing
9. the unemployment rate
10. to reclaim land
11. as a last resort / in the last resort
12. economic power
13. to make a statement
14. to redevelop / renovate the old town
15. to produce a film

Section J

A.
1. pretending / malingering
2. decent / respectable
3. ring-road
4. patio
5. Department
6. anti-social
7. beautifully / supremely well
8. peeping Toms / voyeurs
9. mindless / monotonous / dull / soul-destroying
10. speedometer
11. din / row / racket
12. fibbing, telling them
13. odd / bizarre; (stronger) ridiculous
14. staple
15. will
16. cataract
17. tracks
18. net curtains

B.
1. sting
2. trick
3. stitch
4. stitches
5. lurch
6. bite
7. stab
8. prick
9. engraving

C.
avenge	-	take revenge for
broadcast	-	transmit
chicane	-	device in motor-racing
claim back	-	reclaim
complain	-	moan
despatch	-	send
hand in one's notice	-	resign
pay s.o. back	-	take revenge on s.o.
pay	-	salary
plan	-	scheme
tariff	-	tax

The odd couple is: be resigned and bloody-mindedness

D.
1. 3/4 time
2. a box of chocolates
3. a fair / reasonable / decent offer
4. a spanner
5. a seminar about nuclear power stations
6. to benefit from the course
7. to appeal
8. Where are these cars assembled? / Where does the assembly of these cars take place?
9. Do you take evaporated milk in your tea?
10. a pompous idiot
11. a spur / incentive
12. You have to sign right at the bottom please
13. I feel giddy / dizzy.
14. The applications are piling up.

Section K

A. 1. F - a ti<u>c</u>
    2. T
    3. F - ...a waistcoat (not in AmE!)
    4. F - It is an alloy.
    5. F - Fans can help ....
    6. T
    7. T - But remember tutors are lecturers, not students
    8. T
    9. F - ...go to the polls.
    10. F - A virtuous person ...
    11. T
    12. T
    13. F - Swap *censure* and *censor* and the sentence is correct.
    14. T
    15. F - civilian clothes
    16. F - a chorus which is repeated.

B. a. tact   *(15) diplomacy*
    b. scurrilous   *(9) obscenely abusive; containing obscene humour*
    c. virtuous   *(1) full of virtue*
    d. vital   *(2) essential*
    e. solid   *(16) not hollow*
    f. pimple   *(6) spot*
    g. staple   *(17) fasten together*

C. 1. That takes a heavy toll.
    2. At Christmas there's enormous hustle and bustle in the centre.
    3. Have you overslept? / Did you oversleep?
    4. Would you like to sleep on the problem?
    5. Is this jug made of pure tin? (One would not talk about 'pure pewter'.)
    6. She suffers from glaucoma.
    7. He's just doing his community service.
    8. Is he actually wearing a vest under his waistcoat?
    9. You always have to quote from Shakespeare!
    10. Twenty marks for a tin like that? That really is disgusting / outrageous!

Section L - Test

1. (C) heart
2. (A) degraded
3. (B) a shop
4. (C) happen
5. (B haddock
6. (B) raisin
7. (B) setting fire to buildings
8. (A) denomination
9. (D) writing block (writing **pad**)
10. (B) alcoholic drinks
11. (B) indifferent
12. (A) gargling
13. (B) lenient
14. (B) make a note of
15. (D) crimson
16. (C) a mixer
17. (B) finale
18. (D) all of the last three
19. (C) lawyers
20. (A) goal
21. (B) your conscience
22. (D) props
23. (B) restlessly
24. (A) carry on with
25. (A) garage
26. (B) sponge biscuit
27. (D) helm
28. (B) gigolo
29. (A) old people's home
30. (C) patron
31. (A) policy
32. (A) reason
33. (B) guest-house
34. (B) worthlessness
35. (A) sideburns
36. (C) shrimp
37. (A) adder
38. (C) tribunes
39. (D) muscle

40. (A) nag
41. (C) flick it
42. (B) a genius
43. (D) flutter
44. (A) prank
45. (C) scholarship
46. (C) a spiral
47. (D) wildlife park
48. (C) rash
49. (D) a J.C.B.
50. (C) sparkle

Final Test

FALSE FRIEND	CORRECTION	FALSE FRIEND	CORRECTION
1. disposes of	has / has at its disposal	31. Seminar	Department
2. mundane	sophisticated	32. coursebook	timetable
3. gratifications	bonuses	33. not...human	inhuman
4. feudal	posh / fancy	34. solid	respectable / decent
5. spanner	peeping Tom	35. criminality	crime
6. arson	arsenic	36. prominence	V.I.P.s / top people
7. flipper	pinball machine		
8. resonance	response	37. race	breed
9. callboys	male prostitutes	38. loud	noisy
10. manifest	manifesto	39. absolved	did / took
11. alcoholics	alcohol	40. transparents	banners
12. not social	socially divisive	41. resigned	gave up
13. testament	will	42. swimming	at a loss / lost
14. resume	sum up / summarise	43. stationary	hospital
15. boxes	loudspeakers	44. double	stand-in
16. range	rank	45. Gurgling	Gargling
17. treasure	safe / bank vault	46. basis	grass roots / rank and file
18. exercise	practise		
19. heal	cure	47. mine	refill
20. requisites	props	48. lexicon	dictionary
21. capacities	experts	49. expedition	dispatch department
22. hymn	anthem	50. register	index
23. moment	factor	51. accord work	piece work
24. cloister	monastery	52. simulating	pretending / malingering
25. flint	(shot)gun		
26. confession	denomination	53. resort	department
27. blue-eyed	naive	54. personal	personnel
28. corn	grain	55. branch	trade
29. swindling	fibbing / telling fibs	56. existence	livelihood
		57. tachometer	speedometer
30. demonstratively	pointedly	58. spiral	coil / (less often in conversation) I.U.D.

FALSE FRIEND	CORRECTION	FALSE FRIEND	CORRECTION
59. fete	party	70. trick films	cartoons
60. reclaiming	complaining	71. whirlpool	jacuzzi
61. attest	medical certificate	72. liquid	solvent
62. sonny boy	Prince Charming	73. householder	housekeeper
63. animator	rep / host	74. sets	place mats / tablemats
64. flair	atmosphere	75. tangent	ring road / bypass
65. mode	fashion	76. plastic	sculpture
66. tick	thing	77. fusion	merger
67. spot	ad / commercial	78. sanitize	make ... profitable
68. has got two weeks house arrest	is being kept in for two weeks	79. commanding	ordering ... about
		80. constellation	situation
69. communes	local authorities		

INDEX

The following is a complete index of false friends and pseudo-anglicisms covered in all three volumes in this series, listed by German headword. Where a simple number appears, e.g. '3', it denotes that the word is to be found in alphabetical order in the main body of that volume. Where a letter follows, e.g. '3L', it denotes that the entry is *not* in the main alphabetical body of entries, but in a special section near the beginning or end of that volume: the letter shows you which section. Such special sections occur only in Books 1 and 3.

absolvieren	3	Arsen	3L	Büchse	2
Achsel	3L	Attest	3	Büro	1
adäquat	2	attestieren	3	Callboy	3M
Adreßbuch	3L	ausländisch	2	Camping-Platz	3M
Affekt	2	Automat	3L	Caravan	3M
Aggregat	3	Autoskooter	3M	catchen	3M
agil	3L	Autostop	3M	Catcher	3M
Agonie	3L	baden	1	checken	3M
Aircondition	3M	Bagger	3L	Chef	1
Airfresh	3M	Bandage	3	Chesterkäse	3M
Akademiker(in)	3	Bank	1A	Chips	3M
Akkord	3	Bann	3	Chor	3
akkurat	3	bannen	3	Christ	3L
Akt	2	Baracke	2	Christentum	3L
Akte	2	Barkeeper	3M	City	3M
Akteur	3	Basis	3	Clan	3M
Aktion	1	Beefsteak	3M	Clinch	3M
aktuell	1	bekommen	1	Clique	3
alarmieren	1	Biest	3	Clou	2
Alibi	2	bigott	3	Container	3M
Alkoholika	3L	Biskuit	3L	Crack	3M
Allee	2	Blackout	3M	Crux	3
Allround-man	3M	blamieren	1	Damm	3
Allüren	3	blank	3	Dancing	3M
Ambulanz	2	blauäugig	3L	Dealer	3M
Angina	3L	Blende	3	defilieren	3L
Animateur(in)	3	blenden	3	definitiv	3
animieren	3	blinken	2	degradieren	3L
Annonce	1	Block	3L	Dekorateur(in)	3
Antenne	2	blubbern	3L	Dekoration	3
antik	3	blutig	3	dekorieren	3
Antiquität	3	bohren	2	delikat	3
apart	2	Boiler	3M	dementiert	2
Apparat	2	Bowle	2	demolieren	3
Appartement	2	Box	3M	demonstrativ	3
Appell	3L	Brain-Trust	3M	Depot	3L
Argument	3L	Branche	3	Derby	3M
Armband	3L	brav	1	Desinteresse	3L
Aroma	3L	bringen	1	desinteressiert	3L
arrangieren	2	Brot	2	Devisen	3L
Arrest	3	Brust	2	dezent	2

diagonal,		Flipper	3M	heilen	3
Diagonal-	3L	Flirt	3M	Helm	3L
dick	1	Flug	1A	Hering	3L
differenziert	3	Flur	2	hindern	3
Direktion	2	Folklore	3M	hissen	3L
Direktor(in)	2	fooden	3M	Hitliste	3M
disponieren	3	Form	1	Hochschule	1
Dogge	3L	Format	3	Hometrainer	3M
Dom	2	Fotograf(in)	1	honorieren	3
Double	3	Fraktion	2	Hose	1A
Drache(n)	3	frankieren	3	Hosteß	3M
Drachenflieger	3L	Freak	3M	human	3
Dreß	3M	Frequenz	3	Humor	2
Dressman	3M	Freund(in)	1	Hymne	3L
Drops	3M	frivol	3	Indikation	3
Ebbe	3	frontal, Frontal-	3	Initiative	2
Echo	2	Fusion	3L	inserieren	3
Effekten	3L	Gag	3M	Insider-Tip	3M
egal	1A	Gangsterboß	3M	Inspektion	3
engagiert	1	Garage	3L	Instanz	3
enorm	3	Gasthaus	3L	Intelligenz	3
Etikett	2	Gastronomie	3L	irritieren	1
eventuell	1	genial	2	isoliert	1
Evergreen	3M	Genie	3L	Jacke	2
exaltiert	3L	Gift	1A	Jalousie	3L
Exemplar	1	Glas	1	jobben	3M
exemplarisch	3	Goalgetter	3M	Jubiläum	3
exerzieren	3	Golf	3	jüngste(r,s)	2
Exhibitionist(in)	3	Grad	1	Jury	3M
Existenz	3	grandios	3	Justiz	3
Exkursion	3	Gratifikation	3L	Kabel	2
Expedition	3	graziös	3	Kabine	2
Expertise	3L	Grill	2, 3M	Kalender	2
Exposé	3	grillen	2	Kanal	2
extra	1	grinsen	3	Kanalisation	2
extravagant	3	Gully	3M	Kanne	2
Fabrik	1A	gurgeln	3L	Kanone	3
Facelifting	3M	Gymnasium	1	Kapazität	3
familiär	1	hacken	3	Kapelle	3L
fatal	3	halb (sechs)	1	Karikatur	3
faul	1A	Ham and eggs	3M	Karneval	3
Fest	1	handeln	1	Karte	1
Fete	3	Happy-End	3M	Karton	2
fett	1	Haus	1	Kasino	3L
feudal	3	Hausarbeit	1	Kasse	1
Fieber	3	hausen	3	Kassette	3L
Figur	3	hausieren	3	Kaution	2
Finale	3L	Haushalt	3	Keks	1
Flair	3	Haushälter(in)	3	Kern	3
flattern	3L	Hausmann	3	kicken	3M
flicken	3L	Hausmeister(in)	3	kippen	3L
Flinte	3L	heftig	3	Kipper	3L

Kitt	3	Lektüre	2	Nacken	3L
klappen	3	lernen	2	nagen	3L
Kloster	3L	Lexikon	3	nämlich	3
kochen	1	Libelle	3L	Natur	2
Kombination	2	Lift	3M	necken	3L
kombinieren	2	liften	3M	Nektar	3L
Komfort	2	lila	2	nervös	2
komfortabel	2	Limone	3L	nobel	3
komisch	1	liquide	3L	No-Name(-Produkt)	3M
Komma	3	Lokal, lokal	3	Note	1
kommandieren	3	Looping	3M	notieren	3L
Kommando	3	Lust	1A	Notiz	1
Kommission	3	Make-up	3M	notorisch	3
Kommode	3L	managen	3	Nougat	3
Kommune	3	Manchester	3M	Novelle	3
kompetent	3	Mandat	3	Objekt	3L
Kondensmilch	3	Manifest	3L	Objektiv	3L
Kondition	1	Mann	1A	Obligation	3L
Konfektion	3	Mappe	1	Occasion	1
Konfession	3L	Marine	3L	Ofen	2
Konkurrent(in)	1	Marke	1	offensiv	3
Konkurs	2	markieren	3	offiziös	3L
konsequent	1	Marmelade	1	Oldtimer	3M
Konsequenz	1	Maschine	2	open-end	3M
Konserve	3	massiv	1	ordinär	1
Konstellation	3	Medaillon	3	Organ	3L
Konstrukteur(in)	3	meinen	1	Orientierung	2
Konstruktion	3	Melone	3L	Otter	3L
kontrollieren	1	Menü	2	Paket	2
konzentriert	3	Merry Old England	3M	Palette	3
Konzept	3	Messe	3	Pamphlet	3M
Konzern	3L	Milan	3L	Panne	1A
Konzert	3	mild	3L	Pantomime	2
Konzession	3L	Mimik	3	Paragraph	3
Korn	3	Mine	3	Parkett	3L
Korrespondent(in)	3	Minigolf	3M	Parole	3
Kostüm	3	Misere	3	Partei	3
Koteletten	3L	Mist	1A	Partie	3
Krabbe	3L	Moderator(in)	2	Passage	3L
Krawatte	2	Mode	3	patent	3
Kreuzung	1	Moment	3	pathetisch	2
Kriminalität	3	mondän	3	Patrone	3L
Kritik	1	Montage	3	Pause	1
Küche	1	montieren	2	pedantisch	1
Kur	3	Moor	3	penetrant	3
Kurs	1	Moorhuhn	3L	Pension	1
Kursbuch	3L	Moral	2	perfekt	2
Land	3	Mörder(in)	1	Perle	3
Landschaft	3	Motiv	3L	personell	3
last not least	3M	Motor	3L	Perspektive	2
laut	3	Muschel	3L	Pest	2
Lebensraum	2	Musikbox	3M	Petroleum	3L
leihen	1	nächste(r,s)	1	Pflaster	3

Phantasie	1	puzzeln	3L	scharf	1	
Physiker(in)	2	Puzzle	3M	Schellfisch	3L	
Pickel	3	Qualm	3L	Schema	3	
picken	3L	Quartier	3L	Schikane	3	
pink	3M	Queue	3L	schizophren	3	
Plage	2	quittieren	3	schmal	1	
Plane	3	Quote	3	schwimmen	3	
Plastik	3	Radiorecorder	3M	schwindeln	3	
Platz	1	raffiniert	3	Schnake	2	
Playback	3M	Rakete	3	Schnecke	2	
plump	2	rangieren	3	See	1	
Pointe	2	rasch	3L	Seite	1	
Police	3L	Rasse	3	Sekret	3L	
Politik	3	Rate	2	selbstbewußt	1	
pompös	3	Ratio	3L	selbstgemacht	2	
Pony	3M	rationell	3L	Sellerie	3L	
Porzellan	3L	realisieren	3	Seminar	3	
Potenz	3	rechnen	2	senden	3	
Prädikat	3	reell	3	Sender	3	
prägnant	2	referieren	3	Senior(in)	2	
Praline	3	Reformhaus	3L	sensibel	1	
Prämie	3	Register	3	Serie	2	
Pranke	3L	reklamieren	3	seriös	2	
Präservativ	2	rentabel	1	Sets	3M	
prekär	3L	Rente	1	Shakehands	3M	
prickeln	3L	repräsentativ	2	Shower	3M	
primitiv	2	requirieren	3L	Showmaster	3M	
prinzipiell	2	Requisiten	3L	simulieren	3	
Probe	3	Reservation	3L	Skooter	3M	
proben	3	resignieren	3	skrupellos	2	
profan	3	Resonanz	3	skurril	3	
Profil	2	Ressort	3	Slip	3M	
profitieren	3	Rest	1	Slipper	3M	
Programm	2	restlos	3L	Smoking	3M	
Prominenz	3	resümieren	3L	solide	3	
Promotion	2	revanchieren	3	Sonnyboy	3M	
proper	3	Revision	3	Soße	2	
Prospekt	1	Rezept	1	souverän	3	
Protokoll	3	Rinde	3	sozial	3	
Provision	2	ringen	3L	Spanner	3	
Prozeß	1	Roastbeef	3M	sparen	1	
prüfen	1	Roller	3L	Spektakel	3	
psychisch	2	Roman	1A	spenden	2	
Publikum	1	Rosine	3L	spendieren	2	
Pudding	3M	routiniert	2	Spirale	3L	
Pullunder	3M	Rowdy	3M	Spleen	3M	
Punchingball	3M	Rubrik	3	Spot	3M	
Punker	3M	Salat	1	Spur	3	
Punkt	2	sanieren	3	Stadium	1	
punktuell	3	Sanierung	3L	stapeln	3	
Puppe	3	sauer	2	Star	3	
pur	2	Schal	1	Start	2	
purpur	3L	Schale	3	starten	2	

Station	1, 2	temperamentvoll	1	Unternehmer	1
stationär	3L	Tempo	2	unterwegs	2
steppen	3M	Terminus	3L	unverschämt	3
Stich	3	Terrasse	3	Urne	3
Stipendium	3L	Testament	3	Vasektomie	3L
Stock	1A	Textbuch	3L	Vehikel	3
Stoff	1	Thema	1	Ventilator	3
stoppen	3L	Tick	3	virtuos	3
Store	3	tippen	2	vital	3
streng	1	Ton	2	Vokale	1
Strom	1	Torf	3	Wagen	2
Stuhl	1A	Trainer	3M	wandern	1
stupide	3	trampen	3M	wanken	3L
Sturm	2	Transparent	3L	Warenhaus	1
Subvention	3L	transpirieren	3L	warm	1
süffisant	3L	Tresor	3L	Weg	1
Suggestivfrage	2	Tribüne	3L	Weib	1
surfen	3M	Tribut	3	Wein	3
sympathisch	1	Trickfilm	3L	wenn	1A
synchronisieren	1	trimmen	2	Weste	3
Tablett	1	Trubel	3	Whirlpool	3M
Tachometer	3	Tutor(in)	3	winken	1
Tafel	1A	Twen	3M	Wunder	2
Takt	3	Typ	1	Zensur	3
Talkmaster	3M	überhören	2	Zinn	3
Tangente	3	überschlafen	3	Zirkel	3L
Tarif	3	übersehen	2	zitieren	3
Technik	2	Übersicht	3	zivil, Zivil-	3
Techniker(in)	2	Unterarm	3L	Zylinder	3L
Teens	3M				

NOTES

NOTES